PHILOSOPHY AND
SCIENTIFIC REALISM

International Library of Philosophy and Scientific Method

EDITOR: TED HONDERICH

A Catalogue of books already published in the
International Library of Philosophy and Scientific Method
will be found at the end of this volume.

PHILOSOPHY AND SCIENTIFIC REALISM

by

J. J. C. Smart

Hughes Professor of Philosophy, University of Adelaide

LONDON

ROUTLEDGE & KEGAN PAUL

NEW YORK : THE HUMANITIES PRESS

First published 1963
by Routledge & Kegan Paul Ltd.
Broadway House, 68-74 Carter Lane
London, EC4V 5EL

Second impression 1965
Third impression 1966
Fourth impression 1971

Printed in Great Britain by
Fletcher & Son Ltd, Norwich

ISBN 0 7100 3617 5

CONTENTS

PREFACE   *page* vii

I. THE PROVINCE OF PHILOSOPHY
    Philosophy and World View   1
    Philosophy and the Elimination of Nonsense   3
    Philosophy as more than the Elimination of
        Nonsense   8
    Synoptic Philosophy and Man's Place in Nature   13

II. PHYSICAL OBJECTS AND PHYSICAL THEORIES
    Two Sorts of Phenomenalism   16
    Phenomenalism about Macroscopic Objects   18
    Phenomenalism about Sub-microscopic Objects   27

III. PHYSICS AND BIOLOGY
    The Nature of the Biological Sciences   50
    Psychology   61

IV. THE SECONDARY QUALITIES
    Is Physicalism Adequate?   64
    Criticisms of Two Philosophical Views about
        Colours   66
    Positive Philosophical Theory of Colour   75
    Other Secondary Qualities   85

V. CONSCIOUSNESS
    The Limitations of Behaviouristic Analysis   88
    The Brain Process Theory   92

VI. MAN AS A PHYSICAL MECHANISM
    Men and Mechanisms   106
    Mechanisms and Machines   107
    Problem-solving Ingenuity   111

CONTENTS

The Argument from Gödel   *page* 116
An Inductive Machine   119
Creativity and Freedom   120

VII. THE SPACE–TIME WORLD

Anthropocentric Cosmologies   131
Anthropocentricity of Some Temporal Concepts   132
The Space–Time World   132
The Temporal Asymmetry of the World   142
Conclusion   148

VIII. MAN AND NATURE

Two Sorts of Anthropocentricity   149
Materialism and Values   152

INDEX   157

vi

PREFACE

IN recent years I have been moving away from a roughly neo-Wittgensteinian conception of philosophy towards a more metaphysical one, according to which philosophy is in a much more intimate relation to the sciences. Philosophy, it now seems to me, has to do not only with unravelling conceptual muddles but also with the tentative adumbration of a world view. I have tried to do something of this latter sort in the present book. Though this book is addressed primarily to professional philosophers and students of philosophy, I hope that it may appeal to readers with scientific interests who have not had a specialised philosophical education.

Some parts of this book are based on articles which I have had published in various philosophical journals. However, much of this material has been rewritten. I am grateful to the editors of journals who have allowed me to use this material: a list of acknowledgments will be found on another page.

I wish to thank Dr D. M. Armstrong, Mr Gregory O'Hair, and especially Professor A. G. N. Flew, who have read an earlier draft of this book and who have helped me with their advice and encouragement. In revising this draft I have also been helped by the assistant editor of the International Library of Philosophy and Scientific Method, Mr Bernard Williams. I have had helpful discussions on parts of the book with my colleagues in Adelaide, Dr C. B. Martin (who incidentally suggested the title) and Mr M. C. Bradley. Though we disagree greatly on many issues, for nearly ten years I have been more influenced by Dr Martin's subtle profundities than will be apparent to many readers of this book: in particular, he has done much to wean me from a too positivistic and verificationist way of thinking. I am grateful to Mr and Mrs S. E. Hughes, who have helped with the proof reading, and to Mrs Bartesaghi, who typed the manuscript.

J.J.C.S.

University of Adelaide
South Australia
May 1963

ACKNOWLEDGEMENTS

SEVERAL pages of Chapter II are taken, with slight changes, from my article 'The Reality of Theoretical Entities', *Australasian Journal of Philosophy*, Vol. 34, 1956, pp. 1–12. The first part of Chapter III consists mainly of my article 'Can Biology be an Exact Science?' *Synthese*, Vol. 11, 1959, pp. 359–68. Much of Chapter IV consists, with some interpolations, of my article 'Colours', *Philosophy*, Vol. 36, 1961, pp. 128–42. For part of Chapter V (as well as a page or so of Chapter I) I have made use of my article 'Sensations and Brain Processes', *Philosophical Review*, Vol. 68, 1959, pp. 141–56. Chapter V also makes use of discussion notes, 'Further Remarks on Sensations and Brain Processes', *Philosophical Review*, Vol. 70, 1961, pp. 406–7, 'Sensations and Brain Processes: A Rejoinder to Dr Pitcher and Mr Joske,' *Australasian Journal of Philosophy*, Vol. 38, 1960, pp. 252–4, and 'Brain Processes and Incorrigibility', *Australasian Journal of Philosophy*, Vol. 40, 1962, pp. 68–70. However this chapter has been considerably rewritten. Two paragraphs of Chapter VI are based on part of my article 'Ryle on Mechanism and Psychology', *Philosophical Quarterly*, Vol. 9, 1959, pp. 349–55, and part of this chapter is taken from part of my article 'Gödel's Theorem, Church's Theorem and Mechanism', *Synthese*, Vol. 13, 1961, pp. 105–10. A short passage from Chapter VII is closely related to part of my article 'The Temporal Asymmetry of the World', *Analysis*, Vol. 14, 1953–4, pp. 79–83. I should like to thank the editors of these journals for their permission to make use of this material. I wish also to thank the University of Minnesota Press for allowing me to include in Chapter I and in Chapter III short passages which are closely related to two or three pages of my essay 'Philosophy and Scientific Plausibility', in *Problems of Philosophy, Essays in Honor of Herbert Feigl*, Minneapolis (forthcoming).

I

THE PROVINCE OF
PHILOSOPHY

THIS book is meant as an essay in synthetic philosophy, as the adumbration of a coherent and scientifically plausible world view. A good many philosophers would nowadays question the legitimacy of such an endeavour. It will therefore be as well if I say a few words about the nature of philosophy as I conceive it. No one answer can be given to the question 'What is philosophy?' since the words 'philosophy' and 'philosopher' have been used in many ways. Some people, for example, think of philosophy as offering the consolations of a religion, and of the philosopher as a man who receives with equanimity the buffetings of life. This has very little to do with the way in which academic people, including myself, use the word 'philosophy'. I do not feel particularly unqualified to be an academic philosopher because I am not 'philosophical' when I am bowled out first ball at cricket. As I propose to use the word 'philosophy' it will stand primarily for an attempt to think clearly and comprehensively about: (*a*) the nature of the universe, and (*b*) the principles of conduct. In short, philosophy is primarily concerned with what there is in the world and with what we ought to do about it. Notice that I have said both 'to think clearly' and 'to think comprehensively'. The former expression ties up with the prevailing conception of philosophy as linguistic or conceptual analysis, and the latter ties up with another common conception of philosophy as the rational reconstruction of language so as to provide a medium for the expression of total science.*

Thus, a man might analyse biology in a certain way. He might argue, as I shall do, that living organisms, including human beings, are simply very complicated physico-chemical mechanisms. This man might also analyse physics as the ordering and predicting of sense experiences. For the sake of argument let us concede that such a man might be thinking quite clearly in each field. But though he might be thinking clearly, he would not be thinking *comprehensively*. As biologist he would be thinking of man as a mechanism, as very much a part of nature, a macroscopic object interacting with its environment. As physicist, however, he would be thinking of this great world of nature as just a matter of the actual and possible experiences of sentient beings, and so, in a sense, he would be putting nature inside man.† To think comprehensively he would have to discover a way of thought which enabled him to think both as a biologist and as a physicist. Presumably a comprehensive way of thought would be one which brought all intellectual disciplines into a harmonious relationship with one another. It may turn out that there are some realms of discourse, such as theology, which cannot be brought into a harmonious relationship with the various sciences. Any attempt to do so may result in violence to logic or to scientific facts, or may involve arbitrariness and implausibility. (Consider, for example, the implausibility of a theory which asserts that the mechanistic account of evolution by natural selection and mutation is broadly true, but that there is a special discontinuity in the case of man, to whom was super-added an immortal soul.) If this is so, such anomalous branches of discourse will have to be rejected and will not form part of the reconstruction of our total conceptual scheme.

So much, for the moment, about the 'nature of the universe' or 'world view' part of philosophy. Let us now briefly consider the second part of philosophy, which is concerned with the principles of conduct. We shall not be much concerned in this book with

---

* In thinking of philosophy as rational reconstruction of language I have been very much influenced by Hilary Putnam and by W. V. Quine. See, for example, Quine's *Word and Object* (Technology Press of M.I.T. 1960).

† On this point see Chapter II. It is interesting that theoretical physicists, when they venture into philosophy, commonly tend to be phenomenalists, and biologists tend to be materialists.

this part of philosophy, but in the final chapter I shall try to state some of the implications, and some of the non-implications, of my general world view for ethics. As we shall see, and as has been generally recognised in modern philosophy, it is not possible to deduce propositions about what ought to be done purely from propositions about what is the case. It follows that the principles of conduct are by no means unambiguously determined by our general philosophy. Nevertheless, in their laudable objection to those who would deduce ethics from the nature of the world (and in particular to some of those biologists who would base ethics on the theory of evolution and the like) philosophers have tended to obscure the fact that our general philosophical and scientific beliefs may strongly influence our ethical principles. For example, if one of our principles of conduct were that we should do what is commanded by a personal God and if our world view were one which left no place for such a God, then this principle of conduct would have to be given up, or at least we should have to find some other reason for adhering to it. In this book, which will be naturalistic in temper, I do not wish to concern myself with the general question of the legitimacy or illegitimacy of theology. The example of theology was brought up simply to show in a vivid way that metaphysics can be relevant to ethics. We must certainly not jump from the impossibility of deducing 'ought' solely from 'is' to the untenable position that our general philosophical and scientific views have no bearing on our ethical ones.

PHILOSOPHY AND THE ELIMINATION OF NONSENSE

I have been suggesting a conception of philosophy as the attempt to acquire a synoptic view of the world. On this account of philosophy it shares the tentative character of the sciences. We must never think that we have acquired, even in outline, the final truth, for science inevitably provides surprises for us, and we may have to make important revisions of even our most general notions. We may hope, however, that our synoptic account will be nearer to the final truth than is that of common sense. Now in recent years it has been argued in some quarters that in philosophy we are not concerned, as scientists are, with the distinction between truth and falsity, but with that between sense and nonsense. As philosophers, according to this conception, it is not our business to say what the world is in fact like: we must leave this to scientists and historians. What we can do, and what we are by our training peculiarly fitted to do, is to help to ensure that we, together with scientists and historians, at least utter falsehoods: that we and they do not fall into nonsense which has not even achieved the distinction of an intelligible falsehood. Let me illustrate the notion of nonsense by means of an example based on *Alice in Wonderland*.* Suppose that a man came and said that he had seen a miaowing and blinking cat's head which was unattached to a body. I should be disposed in this case to disbelieve the man, and to say that what he told me was *false*. I should feel that I *understood* him: that I knew what it would be like for such an event as he reported to occur, but that I did not believe that any such event ever had or would occur. His report would contradict various secure beliefs that I possessed, particularly in the field of animal physiology. Now let us suppose that the man had reported not that he had seen a cat's head by itself but that he had seen simply a grin by itself. Not even a grinning mouth unattached to a head, but simply a grin all on its own. In this case I should not know what was meant at all. I should not be disposed to say that I understood what the man said, even though I disbelieved in the truth of his report. I should say, rather, that what he said was nonsense, neither true nor false, and so I could not even disbelieve him.

Now it is indubitable that there are sentences which have appeared to be meaningful and which nevertheless have turned out to be nonsense. I shall mention one such sentence in a moment. And so even though the remarks of traditional philosophers (say, about the famous trio of topics, God, Freedom, and Immortality) may not be obvious nonsense, like the report of the catless grin, they may be nonsense all the same.

Here is a sentence, couched entirely in the respectable terminology of pure mathematics, which at first sight may appear to some readers (assuming that they have not encountered it before) to be perfectly meaningful, though perhaps rather dry and abstract. It was first concocted by Bertrand Russell. (Russell's paradox.) The sentence is: 'The class of all classes not members of themselves is a member of itself.' There appear to be plenty of classes of objects which are not members of themselves. The class of criminals is not

* Lewis Carroll, *Alice in Wonderland* (Everyman edition, J. M. Dent, London, 1952), p. 56.

4

a criminal (the police do not have to seek the *class of criminals* after they have arrested all criminals), and the class of football teams in the league is not a further football team. Most classes therefore appear not to be members of themselves. But some classes do appear to be members of themselves: certainly the class of classes does. For is not the class of classes a class? It would therefore seem to be perfectly intelligible to pose the question of whether the class of all classes not members of themselves is or is not one of those classes which are members of themselves. Unfortunately, this question admits neither the answer 'yes' nor the answer 'no'. For if the class of all classes not members of themselves *is* a member of itself, then it follows that it is one of those classes which are *not* members of themselves. And if it is not a member of itself, then it *is* a member of itself. Either way we get a contradiction. It follows that we can neither say that the sentence 'the class of all classes not members of themselves is a member of itself' expresses a truth, nor can we say that it expresses a falsehood. We are forced to conclude that it is meaningless.*

The above paradox is particularly important and instructive, because it shows how unsuspected possibilities of nonsense can break out even in the rigorous and austere terminology of mathematics. For those readers who may not find abstractions about classes to their taste I shall mention a similar, though less important paradox, which may be even more succinctly stated. Consider the sentence 'This sentence is false'. The sentence is about itself. Is it true or false? It can be neither, because if it is true it is false and if it is false it is true. It is important to note that the above paradoxical sentences are not mere contradictions. You can assert the negation of a contradiction. That is, a contradiction is just plain false. '$2 + 2 = 5$' is a contradiction, and so '$2 + 2 \neq 5$' is a truth. Contradictions have their uses, for they occur in proofs by *reductio ad absurdum*. If you can deduce '$2 + 2 = 5$' you

---

* I here neglect the possibility of other ways of dealing with Russell's paradox, such as Zermelo's. The cautious reader should consult the essay 'The Demarcation between Science and Metaphysics' (especially pp. 263–73) in K. R. Popper's *Conjectures and Refutations* (Routledge and Kegan Paul, London, 1963), which came into my hands while this book was in the press. Popper's argument suggests that we should draw a less sharp line between nonsense and falsehood than I have done. This would strengthen the main argument of this chapter, which is that philosophy is concerned with world view.

can normally deduce that the negation of one or other of the premisses is true. I have said 'normally' here, because it is important to use *reductio ad absurdum* methods only when you are reasonably sure of the meaningfulness of the sentence you are trying to prove. If the sentence you are trying to prove is meaningless it may be like one of the paradoxical sentences above and you may be able to deduce a contradiction both from it *and* from its negation. In which case the deduction of a contradiction from its negation does not ensure its truth. This consideration may be of interest to some readers, in that it may throw light on the fact that certain mathematicians, the so-called 'intuitionists', Brouwer and his school, reject proof by *reductio ad absurdum* in circumstances in which classical mathematicians do not. It is, of course, the case that there are sentences which classical mathematicians regard as meaningful and which the intuitionists hold to be meaningless.

The sort of possibility of nonsense to which I have been drawing attention in the last few paragraphs is a subtle and insidious one. Nonsense of a sort has always been recognised: consider 'I married a prime number' and 'Virtue is triangular'. It is an insight of the last fifty years (though foreshadowed by the philosophically subtle humour of Lewis Carroll) that there can be important and non-obvious possibilities of nonsense. This insight was generalised by Wittgenstein and by those much influenced by him into a complete philosophy of philosophy.

It is clear that some technique for recognising non-obvious nonsense is highly desirable, and I should agree that the development and application of such a technique is at least part of the task of philosophy. How does this connect up with my conception of philosophy as the development of a synoptic outlook? Can the elimination of nonsense change our world view? At first sight the answer to this is in the negative. If the nonsense really is nonsense it cannot form part of a world view, even a false one. So it looks as though elimination of nonsense removes dead wood but does not affect the living branches of our knowledge. This answer is, however, too hasty. It may well be that by using nonsensical premisses, in addition to a set A of meaningful ones, we may be able to deduce a set B of meaningful sentences which are not deducible from A alone. I shall show how to deduce the false but meaningful sentence 'The moon is made of green cheese' from the nonsensical sentence 'This sentence is false'. Let us represent the sentence 'This sentence is false' by the symbol '*S*' for short.

From 'This sentence is false' we can deduce 'This sentence is not false'. That is, from *S* we can deduce not-*S*. However, from *S* we can deduce '*S* or the moon is made of green cheese'. But not-*S* (which we have already deduced) together with '*S* or the moon is made of green cheese' enables us to deduce 'The moon is made of green cheese'.

Thus given the nonsense 'This sentence is false' we can deduce that the moon is made of green cheese. We have been able to do this because the nonsense in question issues in a contradiction, and from a contradiction we can, by the method of the last paragraph, deduce any sentence whatever. It is not obvious, however, that all nonsensical sentences issue in a contradiction. Some seem so far off the rails of meaningful discourse that it is not even possible to use them to demonstrate their own senselessness. Thus, it is not obvious that 'I married a prime number' or 'A bodiless grin appeared in the room' issue explicitly in contradiction. Nevertheless, my derivation of the proposition that the moon is made of green cheese should make it plausible that a philosopher should be able to deduce false conclusions from true premisses if he makes his deduction through unrecognised nonsense. The deduction would, of course, be an incorrect one, but it would be incorrect in a very unobvious and subtle way. The detection of its incorrectness would depend on the detection of hidden nonsense. A good example of this sort of thing, in the history of philosophy, suggested to me by D. M. Armstrong, is perhaps Aristotle's deduction of the false, though meaningful, proposition that the heavenly bodies are of a different substance from that of the earth. His deduction is by way of the nonsense that the heavenly bodies obey laws of the same nature as the laws of logic, *i.e.* laws of a sort of logical hardness.

It may be thought that my example of a deduction that the moon is made of green cheese proves too much. For if it proves anything it proves that from 'This sentence is false' (or from a simple non-paradoxical contradiction such as '$2 + 2 = 5$') we could deduce anything whatever. But philosophers, however metaphysical they may be, are not satisfied to assert any proposition whatever. There are some propositions which they wish to assert and there are other propositions which they wish to deny. A system of thought which harboured a contradiction would, on the contrary, degenerate into the happy assertion of anything whatever. To this objection we must reply that in practice a system will degenerate in this way only if the contradiction is detected. If the contradiction is not detected it cannot in practice provide a route for the deduction of any proposition whatever. It is like a way out of prison which is quite unknown to the prisoners:* as far as they are concerned it might as well not exist, and the bolts and bars do not lose any of their effectiveness.

I conclude therefore that it must not be supposed that the view that philosophy consists only in the elimination of nonsense implies the proposition that philosophy has no effect on our world view. It may cause us to shed some of our beliefs about the world because it may enable us to see that we have accepted these beliefs only on the strength of a fallacious deduction through a nonsensical part of language. This conclusion is far stronger than another one, which is conceded by most philosophers, that the elimination of nonsense leads to clarity of thought and so helps the progress of the sciences.

PHILOSOPHY AS MORE THAN THE ELIMINATION OF NONSENSE

That philosophy is at least the elimination of nonsense and the clarification of thought is something of which I have not the least doubt. However, I should also wish to argue that philosophy is more than this, and that it is the business of the philosopher to decide between various synoptic hypotheses on grounds of plausibility. Of course, scientists have to decide between hypotheses, and with a slight over-simplification we may say that they do so by means of observation and experiment. It may be, however, that no available method of experiment and observation will decide between two hypotheses. The philosopher may legitimately, I think, feel it within his province to speculate on the relative plausibilities of the two hypotheses if they are of such generality and importance as to affect our overall world view. For example, in the sequel I shall be concerned to argue for the plausibility of the view that the human brain is no more than a physical mechan-

* I think that this simile is originally due to Wittgenstein.

ism, that no vitalistic or purely psychical entities or laws are needed to account for its operations. This type of philosophical thinking links up closely with the purely clarificatory sort of philosophy since part of my strategy will be to try to expose confusions in *a priori* philosophical arguments for the opposite hypothesis. Of course, those who produce such *a priori* arguments will probably deny that what they are arguing for is a 'hypothesis': they will hold that their view is true as a matter of logic, just as a mathematical proposition perhaps is. I shall, however, indicate why I think that such philosophers are too sanguine in regarding philosophy as pure logic.

A philosopher might have to decide between two hypotheses for which there not only is no available empirical test but for which there could be no possible empirical test. I shall illustrate this point by reference to the hypothesis that the universe began to exist ten minutes before I began writing this sentence, but with everything just as it was ten minutes ago.* (Fossils in the rocks, photographs in the pocket, memory traces in the brain, light rays in interstellar space, and so on.)† Of course this is not a hypothesis which any philosopher is likely to hold, though the English naturalist and biblical theologian Philip Gosse produced a very similar theory in order to reconcile geology and the book of Genesis.‡ Gosse held that the world was created only a few thousand years ago, exactly as stated in the book of Genesis, but that God had also created the various eroded canyons, fossils as if of prehistoric animals and plants, and so on. In short, he held that the world was created a few thousand years ago just as in fact it was (on the usual geological and evolutionary account) at that time. Clearly Gosse's theory was immune to empirical refutation, and he was extremely pained when both the scientific world and the theological world spurned his ingenious reconciliation. Nevertheless, though it is not a live philosophical theory, the hypothesis that the world began ten minutes ago, just as it was

---

* If someone raises the relativistic objection that 'ten minutes ago' has no unambiguous meaning we can say 'ten minutes ago with reference to some specified inertial frame of reference'.

† See Bertrand Russell, *Analysis of Mind* (Allen and Unwin, London, 1921), pp. 159–60.

‡ An interesting account of Philip Gosse's theory is given in Martin Gardner, *Fads and Fallacies in the Name of Science* (Dover Inc., New York, 1957), pp. 124–7.

ten minutes ago, will serve to illustrate my methodological point. It is clear that no experiment or observation could upset the hypothesis that the world began ten minutes ago just as it was ten minutes ago. If I mention our memories of last week's football match the reply will be that these are not true memories: the football match never happened, but we came into existence ten minutes ago complete with pseudo-memories of the non-existent game. If I point to newspaper photographs of the football match the reply will be that the newspaper, complete with photographs, itself began to exist ten minutes ago. And so on.

Some philosophers would say that since there could be no experimental or observational way of deciding the question whether or not the world came into existence ten minutes ago just as it was ten minutes ago, the assertion or denial that the world began ten minutes ago is without sense. This seems to me to be unplausible. There seems to be nothing contradictory in the notion of a world suddenly springing into existence in this way. Moreover, suppose that I am suffering from an intense toothache. I should not take kindly to the view that in a year's time there would be no meaningful difference between the hypothesis that the world exists now, complete with my toothache, and the hypothesis that the world will spring into existence next year, just as it will be next year, with pseudo-traces, such as memories and empty gums, as if of my present toothache.

It is hard, therefore, without losing all sense of reality, to deny that the hypothesis that the world began ten minutes ago just as it was ten minutes ago is a meaningful one. (Though an unbelievable one.) Indeed, though there are no possible observations or experiments which could distinguish between this hypothesis and the more usual one, there are considerations, hard though they may be to formulate, of simplicity and plausibility, which should determine us to reject the 'ten minutes ago' hypothesis. For this hypothesis presents us with a cosmology depending on a highly complex and arbitrary set of initial conditions. If the 'ten minutes ago' hypothesis is accepted, then we have to take as a brute fact, for which no explanation could possibly be given, that ten minutes ago there were certain footprints on the beach at Glenelg, South Australia, that there were certain light waves in the depths of intergalactic space, that there were certain definite 'photographs' in my breast pocket, that there were certain types of pseudo-prehistoric bones in the rock strata.* All these facts would have to be taken as just 'flat' and in principle inexplicable. Now it is true that on any hypothesis there is an element of arbitrariness in nature. Why have we five fingers rather than four or six? Nevertheless this arbitrariness can be understood as due to the element of sheer accident involved in the large-scale non-accident of evolution by natural selection. This arbitrariness, and other sorts of arbitrariness, such as the occurrence of hard rocks here and soft rocks there, of blue stars here and red stars there, is, on the normal hypothesis that the world has existed for a very long time, much what we should expect. It would be surprising rather if everything were neat and orderly. But this sort of arbitrariness is not like the extraordinary and universal arbitrariness of the initial conditions which we find in the 'ten minutes ago' hypothesis.

The example of the hypothesis that the universe began to exist ten minutes ago seems to show that it is possible to choose, on grounds of plausibility, between two hypotheses between which there can be no empirical test. I shall myself consider one important case of this sort in a later chapter, when I shall argue for the view that our conscious experiences are to be *identified* with brain processes. Another possible view would be that our conscious experiences are not identical with brain processes but that they are *correlated* with brain processes. Here once more we have, as we shall see, two hypotheses between which no empirical test could decide. I shall argue on plausible grounds for the former (materialistic) hypothesis against the latter (dualistic) hypothesis. Before I can do this I shall, of course, have to argue that certain *a priori* philosophical arguments against materialism are not so cogent as they seem at first sight to be. The plausible arguments I shall use are of various sorts, but one of these is worthy of specific mention. This is *Occam's razor*. It depends on the precept 'Do not multiply entities beyond necessity'. This is a familiar maxim not only of philosophical method but also of scientific method. For example, if biochemical reactions will explain a certain phenomenon of cell growth, then there is no need to postulate, in addition to the biochemical reactions which we know to occur anyway, a life force or some irreducibly biological law of nature. (Occam himself is popularly supposed to have applied his razor to the meta-

* I am also neglecting the arbitrariness of our choice of criterion of simultaneity at a distance, which is implied by the special theory of relativity.

physical problem of universals, though I gather that there is a good deal of doubt about the historical accuracy of this.) It might turn out that in cases where we need to talk of universals, such as justice and whiteness, we could manage equally well by talking of the *words* 'just' and 'white'. If we can think of words as marks on paper and the like (the trouble, of course, is that words, unlike particular inscriptions, themselves turn out to be universals), then we can effect an economy. For we know that ink marks on paper and the like occur anyway, and if they will do all the explanatory tasks that are needed we need not bring in the airy fairy and altogether dubious entities justice and whiteness.

I suspect that considerations of plausibility, turning on the notions of simplicity and arbitrariness, of Occam's razor and the like, have an important and indeed indispensable place in philosophical argument. This is partly because philosophy is carried out in a natural language, not in some artificial language, with rigid formation and transformation rules explicitly laid down as in a formal logical or mathematical system. Hence, though it is often possible to *persuade* another philosopher that he has landed himself in inconsistency or in nonsense, and that he must therefore give up certain of his tenets, it is never possible to *prove* this to him. He can always patch up the inconsistencies and nonsenses in his language by means of supplementary rules and hypotheses. We shall have to present an alternative in Chapter 6 to the so-called libertarian theory of free-will. At first sight this theory is easy to refute, for the libertarian seems to hold that acting freely is something intermediate between being determined and acting by pure chance. Logic would seem to leave no room for such an intermediate possibility. The libertarian will reply that if I define 'pure chance' as 'not being determined', then his 'acting freely' is a sub-species of what I call 'pure chance'.* This sub-species is not properly pure chance, but consists in acting from reasons, not from causes. I then reply to the libertarian with the stock philosophical arguments showing that reasons are not a sort of para-cause and that acting from reasons is not incompatible with acting from

---

* This paragraph was already written and set up in print before I saw the two lucid notes by Richard Acworth and C. A. Campbell in *Mind*, Vol 72, 1963, pp. 271–2 and 400–5. These reply to a former article of mine and point out that the libertarian could defend himself by partitioning the field which I call 'pure chance'.

causes. The obdurate libertarian is sure to prepare yet another line of defence and get round this objection in some way. (As I well know from inconclusive philosophical discussions on this topic.)

This characteristic inconclusiveness of philosophical argument is a fact familiar to all philosophers. If they were to take it seriously more of them would be favourably disposed to my conception of philosophy as in part depending on merely plausible considerations. If a philosopher keeps on patching up his theory we may try to persuade him that his way of talking is becoming more and more baroque and is ill-fitting to our scientific knowledge. The libertarian philosopher of free-will may, if he is ingenious enough, render himself immune to our logical arguments, but only at the cost of great artificiality in his theory, and at the price of bringing in a great discontinuity in the story of animal evolution. Just where in the line of evolution, the primates, or sub-men, or early men, does this 'soul', or power of free choice in the libertarian sense, become superadded to man as he appears in the usual biological story? It would, moreover, have to be a very special creation: it is impossible that the evolution of such a metaphysical entity could be explained in the usual mechanistic terms, natural selection acting on gene pools (a gene being a complex nucleic acid). Of course, if the philosopher is happy with the baroque quality of his theory and with its artificiality of fit with total science, then there is no more to be done. In many cases, however, plausible considerations of the sort I have suggested may have a persuasive force that purely abstract considerations of consistency and the like may not have. With ingenuity these last can be got round, but if the methods of getting round them have to be supplemented every century, or every decade, in order to take account of advances in science, then it will be a very romantically minded philosopher who will not begin to feel uneasy.

SYNOPTIC PHILOSOPHY AND MAN'S PLACE IN NATURE

If philosophy is concerned, in the manner suggested above, with the rational reconstruction of our conceptual scheme, then it quite obviously covers a very wide field.* There will therefore be

* W. V. Quine has recently argued against the tenability of the analytic-synthetic distinction. (See his *Word and Object, op. cit.*, also his *From a Logical Point of View* (Harvard University Press, 1953).) According to this laws

some important issues which, for the purposes of this book, I shall be content to leave to one side. For example, I shall not be concerned with the much-vexed question of Platonism versus nominalism, that is, whether in addition to the concrete objects or events which exist in space and time we must postulate abstract objects as well. For example, do mathematicians assert the reality of *numbers* and *classes*? The two parts of the previous question can indeed be amalgamated if we accept Frege's and Russell's analysis of numbers as classes of classes of objects. In any case, in higher mathematics it is essential to introduce infinite classes, *i.e.* classes of numbers. That a class is an abstract object can most easily be seen if we consider the null class, which can be described, *e.g.*, as the class of twentieth-century terrestrial unicorns. The null class is a perfectly good class, and because it has no members there is no temptation to confuse it with the 'heap' of its members. A class, unlike a heap, has a number. Consider the class of students who are in this room at a certain moment. It has, say, 10 members. Contrast the spatially scattered 'heap' of human protoplasm in this room. This has no number. It is made up of 10 persons and 10^{15} living cells and goodness knows how many molecules or atoms.* Now science, since it includes mathematics, apparently has to mention classes. Does this mean that we must accept classes as real things postulated by science, on a par, perhaps, with

* Cf. W. V. Quine, *From a Logical Point of View* (Harvard University Press, 1953), p. 114.

of logic and of pure mathematics are not different in kind from very high level laws of physics. It would also seem to follow from his view that there would be an arbitrariness in the formation rules which we lay down for a system. Indeed, there are varying expedients in mathematical logic to eliminate the class of all classes paradox, and some sentences which would be meaningless in Whitehead and Russell's system are allowed in Quine's *Mathematical Logic* (Harvard University Press, 1958). There is perhaps a certain arbitrariness in whether we regard something as meaningless or as a high-level falsehood. (Thus, it could be taken not as meaningless that there are catless grins, but that it follows from certain very high level assumptions that there are none.) If Quine's views on the nature of logic are accepted, then the first of the two conceptions of philosophy that I have sketched in this chapter collapses into the second. If so, this only strengthens my position in this book. Since Quine's views are controversial, I do not wish to commit myself on this issue, which is a highly technical one, and which would in any case lead us away from the main preoccupations of this book. See also footnote to p. 5.

electrons or the far side of the moon ?* The reason why I shall not discuss this issue of Platonism versus nominalism, or of the reality of abstract entities, is that it has little relevance to the question of man's place in the universe. The connecting theme of this book will be the attack on anthropocentric or near-anthropocentric strains of thought in philosophy. I shall attack phenomenalist and subjectivist theories of mind and matter, space and time. The question of whether the universe contains Platonic entities is neutral to these issues.

Of course, the days when man was thought to be physically at the centre of the universe are long over, but as I shall try to show, a disguised anthropocentricity still prevails in many fields of philosophy. For example, traditional phenomenalism in a sense puts this great world of nature 'inside sentience': indeed, as we shall see, phenomenalism has appealed to no less a man than F. P. Ramsey on account of its apparent power to tame the vast astronomical spaces that threatened to overawe him. Moreover, I shall be concerned to refute the more recent phenomenalism, not of tables and chairs but of electrons and protons, which has attempted to deny the full-blooded reality of the sub-microscopic world, *i.e.* of objects of an order of magnitude very much smaller than those of macroscopic or roughly man-sized objects. In later chapters I shall attack anthropocentricity in prevailing theories of the secondary qualities and of consciousness, and I shall be concerned to put man in his place by defending the view that he is nothing more than a complicated physical mechanism. The ground for this part of the book is prepared by a chapter on the relations between physics and biology. The chapter on space and time might be thought to be outside the scope of the book, but the reader will, if he perseveres, discover that even in such notions as of past, present, and future there is a concealed anthropocentricity. In the final chapter there is a discussion of the relevance and lack of relevance of a materialistic metaphysics for ethics.

* For a discussion of this issue see especially Quine, *op. cit.*

II

PHYSICAL OBJECTS AND
PHYSICAL THEORIES

LET us begin by taking it as a fact which does not require further analysis, that the world contains such things as tables, stones, trees, and stars. That is, we shall begin by regarding these things, macroscopic physical objects, as philosophically uncontroversial.* What about the sub-microscopic entities of physical theory, electrons, protons, neutrons, mesons, photons, and the like? Many philosophers would wish to say that these are not so much part of the furniture of the world as useful conceptual devices for predicting the behaviour of macroscopic objects such as stones and galvanometers. On this view, to say that electrons are real is to say no more than that the word 'electron' plays a useful part in certain physical theories which enable us to predict and control events on the macroscopic level. We do not think of nations as anything over and above people, and similarly the physicist's talk about electrons may be no more than a concise way of talking about observations with macroscopic objects such as electroscopes and Wilson cloud chambers. This is the philosophy of science made popular by Ernst Mach and adopted by many physicists when they branch off into philosophy. Moreover, it is, I think, the philosophy which was originally behind (though inessential to) Heisenberg's matrix

* For interesting remarks on the notion of 'the uncontroversial' see Stuart Hampshire's paper 'Interpretation of Language' in *British Philosophy in the Mid-Century*, edited by C. A. Mace (Allen and Unwin, London, 1957).

mechanics, in which the symbolism is designed in such a way that assertions about measurable properties can be made only in those cases in which measurements could in principle be carried out. It certainly seems to lie behind the so-called 'Copenhagen interpretation' of quantum mechanics. Among philosophers, too, this philosophy of science has sometimes seemed so obvious as hardly to be worth stating. For example, a very subtle form of the doctrine is, I think, implicit in John Wisdom's influential series of papers on 'Other Minds'.* On this view the theoretical entities of physics are of the nature of convenient fictions. Tables are not made of protons, electrons, neutrons, etc., in anything like the way in which a wall is made of bricks.

The philosophy of physics which I have adumbrated in the last paragraph, and which I wish to oppose, is in some ways similar to the philosophical doctrine of phenomenalism. This is the view that (as J. S. Mill put it†) matter is 'a permanent possibility of sensation'. In other words, it asserts that statements about chairs and tables come roughly to something of the form 'If such and such sense experiences are had then such and such other sense experiences are had'. The view of the theoretical entities of physics which I wish to attack assumes the reality of macroscopic objects such as tables, chairs, stones, and galvanometers, but regards electrons and the like as 'permanent possibilities' of observations of macroscopic objects. Proponents of this philosophy of physics may or may not be realists about tables, but they are phenomenalists about electrons. Frequently, of course, the two sorts of phenomenalism go together, as with, for example, Mach,‡ Dingle,§ Margenau.‖ If it is supposed that talking about electrons is just a convenient way of talking about galvanometers and cathode-ray tubes, etc., and if it is also supposed that talking about galvanometers and cathode-ray tubes is just a way of talking about our sense experiences, then it will be supposed that talking about

* John Wisdom, *Other Minds* (Blackwell, Oxford, 1952).

† J. S. Mill, 'An Examination of Hamilton's Philosophy', Chapter II in *John Stuart Mill's Philosophy of Scientific Method*, edited by Ernest Nagel (Hafner, New York, 1950). See p. 371.

‡ E. Mach, *The Science of Mechanics*, translated by T. J. McCormack, Sixth Edition (Open Court, La Salle, Illinois, 1960).

§ H. Dingle, *Through Science to Philosophy* (Clarendon Press, Oxford, 1937).

‖ H. Margenau, *The Nature of Physical Reality* (McGraw-Hill, New York, 1950).

electrons is itself just a way of talking about sense experiences. Thus, phenomenalism about theoretical entities goes along neatly with phenomenalism about macroscopic objects. But the two views need not go together. If you are a phenomenalist about galvanometers you have to be a phenomenalist about electrons too, but you can be a realist about galvanometers and a phenomenalist about electrons.

It will be as well to point out that I have been using the epithet 'phenomenalist' rather more widely than some philosophers would like. Some philosophers might say that electrons are not anything 'over and above' the laboratory instruments which provide 'evidence' for them, just as nations are nothing over and above citizens. Nevertheless, they would stress that statements about electrons cannot be *translated* into statements about laboratory instruments, just as statements about England cannot be translated into statements about Tom, Dick, and Harry. There is an indefiniteness in the concept of nation or electron which precludes such a strict translation. Furthermore, such philosophers would stress that nations and electrons are not ordinary fictions, like unicorns, but are 'logical fictions'. That is, there is a sense in which nations and electrons undoubtedly exist. I hope I shall make it clear in the next few pages why I consider such philosophers as, from the ontological point of view, phenomenalists.* The difference between these philosophers and less squeamish philosophers of the phenomenalist sort seems to me to be unimportant compared with the difference between these philosophers and those who, like myself, wish to take an unashamedly realistic view of the fundamental particles of physics.

PHENOMENALISM ABOUT MACROSCOPIC OBJECTS

Phenomenalism about macroscopic objects, though not phenomenalism about submicroscopic ones, has taken a considerable beating in recent years at the hands of British and American philosophers. I shall not therefore spend a great deal of time on its refutation, though I shall indicate what I think is wrong with it. I shall devote more attention to the more controversial task of refuting phenomenalism about submicroscopic objects.

* See also D. M. Armstrong, *Perception and the Physical World* (Routledge and Kegan Paul, London, 1961), pp. 47–50.

Phenomenalism is a modern refinement of a theory put forward by Bishop Berkeley. Berkeley held that when the gardener talks about a cherry, what he is in fact talking about are the sense experiences of colour, sweetness, and so on. The cherry is 'a congeries of perceptions'. Berkeley allowed that the cherry exists when no man or animal is perceiving it, for he held that it is perceived by God. Modern phenomenalism gets over this difficulty without bringing in God: it analyses propositions about the cherry into *hypothetical* propositions about sense experiences. These propositions are to the effect that if certain sense experiences are had, then certain other sense experiences are had. Such a hypothetical proposition can, of course, be true, even when its protasis and apodosis are both false. The truth of such hypothetical propositions about sense experiences as of a cherry guarantees the existence of the cherry even when it is not perceived. Or rather, this account would guarantee the existence of unperceived cherries if it could be made sound against other objections.

Phenomenalism obviously entangles in the difficulties in analysing the so-called 'strong' conditional. There is one very clear sense in which we might use the expression 'if p then q'. This is simply to assert 'not both p and not-q'. Certainly this is *part* of what we normally mean by 'if p then q'. It is hard to see what more can be meant by 'if p then q'. I myself would be prepared to argue, though I shall not do so here, that the so-called 'weak' conditional, where 'if p then q' does just mean 'not both p and not-q', is sufficient for all mathematical and scientific purposes. Quite clearly it is not sufficient for the phenomenalist. When he says that the existence of the unperceived cherry comes to 'if such and such sense experiences were had, then such and such other sense experiences would be had', he does not want this hypothetical to be trivially true because of the falsity of the protasis. It is also true of the unperceived cherry that if (in the sense of the weak conditional) experiences as of the cherry are had, then the sun turns bright purple. The phenomenalist has therefore to give a philosophically adequate account of the strong conditional. I myself do not know of such an account which will take care of the sorts of cases with which the phenomenalist has to deal. For example, a promising suggestion of Reichenbach's will not be good enough for him. This is roughly that 'if p then q' in the strong sense is to be analysed as: ' "Not both p and not-q" is a law in some well-tested body of physical theory or is deducible from such a theory together with some true set of initial conditions.'* For the phenomenalist's analysis does not, and cannot, make reference to such a body of theory. Let us nevertheless for the sake of argument concede to the phenomenalist that he has succeeded in giving a clear analysis of the strong conditional.

One of the difficulties about phenomenalism is that it is by no means easy to give a precise account of what the hypothetical propositions about sense experiences would be like. We may begin by mentioning some difficulties considered by H. H. Price, in his book *Hume's Theory of the External World*.† Consider the statement 'The walls of the bathroom are blue'. At a first shot the phenomenalist might analyse this as 'If I were in the bathroom I would be having blue sense impressions'. But what does 'in the bathroom' mean here? These words would themselves have to be analysed in terms of actual and possible sense impressions. Perhaps we might replace the reference to the bathroom by the phrase 'if I had such and such sense impressions' (*e.g.* of white bath, red tiles, green mat). Our original sentence would then become, say, 'if I had sense impressions as of white bath, red tiles, green mat, then I would have sense impressions as of blue walls'. Even so, our analysis is incomplete. I might have sense impressions as of white bath, red tiles, green mat in a similar bathroom which had yellow walls. Or again, I might be having an hallucination as of seeing white bath, red tiles, and green mat. Price has suggested that 'in the bathroom' might be elucidated by reference to the chain of sense impressions which I would get by moving to the bathroom from wherever I was when I made the statement about the bathroom. (Up the stairs, over the landing, and along the passage, for example.) But once more the same trouble recurs: it will not do, for example, that I should dream or be hallucinated that I move from here to the bathroom. Further 'if . . . then . . .' clauses would have to be put in so as to rule out these possibilities, and it is not evident that this can be done without the whole trouble recurring all over again.

* H. Reichenbach, *Nomological Statements and Admissible Operations* (North-Holland, Amsterdam, 1954).

† H. H. Price, *Hume's Theory of the External World* (Clarendon Press, Oxford, 1940).

Another difficulty in the phenomenalist account, as it has been presented above, is to explain what the word 'I' means in the sentence 'if I were in the bathroom I would have blue sense impressions'. Normally when I say something of the form 'I did so and so' the word 'I' could be replaced by my own name 'Smart'. Now what is Smart? He is at least this, a body that walks and talks. It would seem therefore that on the phenomenalist analysis not only the word 'bathroom' but also the word 'I' would have to be expanded in terms of actual and possible sense impressions. A. J. Ayer, however, has suggested eliminating all reference whatever to the percipient, and to have the analysis in terms of 'if such and such sense impressions are had, then such and such other sense impressions are had'.* He rightly points out (in effect) that the description of the sensory route from 'here–now' to the bathroom ought not to enter into the analysis of 'the walls of the bathroom are blue', since I could understand the proposition about the bathroom without having the least idea of what it would look and feel like to move from here, up the stairs, and along the passage, or whatever the route is.† Ayer also convincingly shows that it is difficult to see how to give a plausible account, on Price's lines, of propositions about events remote in time, for instance, thousands of years before one's own birth. Ayer's solution is not to refer to the observer at all, but simply to 'describe the scenery'. We just analyse material object propositions on the lines of 'if there are (were, will be) such and such sense impressions, then there are (were, will be) such and such other sense impressions'. It is not at all clear to me how Ayer avoids the objection that I might be dreaming or that I might be hallucinating the bathroom, nor is it clear how he could get over the difficulty about the two bathrooms which are precisely similar exept that one has blue walls where the other has yellow ones. Ayer himself uses the example of the South Pole. Now two different places near the South Pole might, especially in a blizzard, look and feel exactly the same, and it might be that magnetometer readings and the like would be indistinguishable too. How would the phenomenalist distinguish these two places? Even if this difficulty can be got over, Ayer's amendment of the theory would clearly have to be stated with great care.

* A. J. Ayer, essay on 'Phenomenalism' in his *Philosophical Essays* (Macmillan, London, 1954).

† Ayer, *ibid.*, p. 156.

Obviously it would not be good enough for the sense impressions which satisfy the protasis of the hypothetical to be sense impressions had by me (in Australia, say) and those which satisfy the apodosis to be sense impressions had by you (in England, say). The sensory relations holding between the sense impressions mentioned in the protasis and those mentioned in the apodosis would have to be carefully specified. So would the relations between sense impressions within either protasis or apodosis alone. What is to prevent my visual sense impressions being grouped with your auditory ones, for example? Moreover, it is difficult to see how reference to the percipient can be avoided in view of such facts as that white paper looks yellow to the man who has jaundice.

It should be becoming increasingly evident that a phenomenalist analysis of even so simple a proposition as that the walls of the bathroom are blue would probably be very complicated, and that it is not even certain that it could be carried out. The theory looks more unplausible and in danger of harbouring hidden inconsistencies than it did at first sight. Fortunately I do not need to go into a consideration of whether (and if so how) phenomenalism might be amended so as to overcome the difficulties of the last few paragraphs, for I think there are objections to any form of phenomenalism. I pass first of all to a strong objection which I owe independently to C. B. Martin and D. M. Armstrong.*

Even a phenomenalist will have to admit that there is no contradiction in the supposition that there might never have been, and never would be, any sentient beings in the universe. If the earth had not been so luckily placed in relation to the sun, or if the sun had been a rather different sort of star, there would have been no life on earth. And though it is now becoming plausible that, scattered throughout the universe, there are innumerable planetary systems which support life, we can certainly imagine that this should not have been so. One surely ought not to be able to prove the existence of life on other worlds purely *a priori*, and there is no doubt that life on our own planet is to some extent a happy accident. We ought therefore to be able to talk intelligibly about a lifeless universe. It is at least a *false* sentence, not a *meaningless* one, that sentient creatures do not exist. Now what can the phenomenalist say about a lifeless universe? The universe, according to

* Martin verbally. For Armstrong see his book (*op. cit.*), pp. 56–8.

him, consists of actual and possible sense impressions. A lifeless universe will consist of possible ones only. The possibilities here are clearly empirical ones, not logical possibilities. But how can one talk of empirical possibilities independently of *all* actualities? Surely the assertion of a possibility can be made only on the basis of an actuality. The possibility that a glass window-pane will break is asserted on the basis of the actual molecular and physical structure of the glass, or alternatively, on the basis that similar panes of glass have broken in the past. The phenomenalist's account of the lifeless universe would have to be in terms of possibilities which are nowhere grounded in actualities, and this seems quite unintelligible.

Armstrong admits that the phenomenalist could dodge this objection simply by accepting its consequence, *i.e.* by taking the heroic course of conceding that a mindless universe would not contain any matter either. (Such a consequence would indeed appeal to a theological apologist such as Berkeley.) Nevertheless, there are further objections based on the same general principle, namely that possibilities must depend on actualities. (I am here indebted to a paper by Wilfrid Sellars.*) A possibility must be based on *actual* regularities. Thus, we can talk about a possible catch if you flick your bat at a ball outside the off stump, but this is because batsmen who have *actually* flicked at balls outside the off stump have got caught. (Or maybe the possibility here could be based on actual observations in psychology and physiology. Notice that 'possible' here does not mean 'logically possible' but 'consistent with the body of one's empirical knowledge'.) Now the phenomenalist has to talk of 'actual and possible' sense impressions. Sellars points out that the realist can easily talk of 'possible' sense-impressions, because he grounds the possibility of getting certain sense impressions partly on certain actual regularities at the level of the material object language. It is easy to see how, on this common-sense level, we could back up our talk about the possibility of getting a sense-impression as of the fire if I open my eyes: we should talk about fires, light rays, eyelids, and so on. How is the phenomenalist to do it? He can back up his talk about possible sense-impressions only by regularities among *actual* sense-impressions.

* 'Phenomenalism' in *Science, Perception and Reality*, Chapter 3 (Routledge and Kegan Paul, London, 1963).

Sellars concedes that such regularities among a given person's sense-impressions do exist, and he dismisses as irrelevant, and concerned with the genetic psychology rather than with the logic of the situation, that these regularities could be *found* only by someone who already could speak of material objects. What he does point out is that these regularities will be *accidental* generalisations, dependent on the peculiarities of my own autobiography and environment. Consider the proposition 'all the beer bottles in this room are empty'. This can be put into the form 'if anything in this room is a beer bottle it is empty'. It does not allow us to make predictions about further bottles in the room, *e.g.* port bottles. It is known to be true only because we have looked at all the beer bottles in the room and have found that, as a matter of fact, they happen all to be empty. Any universal conditional of the form 'such and such of my sense-impressions are followed by such other of my sense-impressions' would be true only accidentally and contingently: for example, that sense-impressions as of a blue mat are surrounded by sense-impressions as of a green floor would be true accidentally only. (If we allow ourselves to talk of material objects for a moment it is because, as a matter of fact, my bath mat is blue and my bathroom floor is green.) In general, regularities among my sense-impressions will depend on accidental facts about my own environment: the sort of furniture that I possess, and so on. It follows that no generalisations about my sense-impressions will possess the non-accidental universality of laws of nature. *A fortiori* this will be true of sense-impressions in general. It is impossible to find non-accidental universal conditionals about sense-impressions, and hence there is nothing to give backing to the notion of a possible sense-impression.*

The philosophical refutation of phenomenalism should be welcomed by those who, like me, regard it as an antecedently implausible doctrine anyway. To say that the great nebula in Andromeda is just a matter of the actual and possible sense impressions of terrestrial and extra-terrestrial observers seems to give to sentience a most unplausible centrality to the scheme of things. And yet it is this very thing which gives phenomenalism a certain attraction to some otherwise hard-boiled philosophers. F. P. Ramsey, had he not died so young, would have profoundly

* For further objections to phenomenalism, see Armstrong, *op. cit.*, Chapters 5 and 6, and Sellars *op. cit.*, Chapter 3.

influenced the course of modern philosophy. Even as it was, his achievements were outstanding. Ramsey would certainly have been classed by William James as one of the 'tough minded' sort of philosopher. And yet, even so, Ramsey seemed abashed by the vast astronomical spaces, by the apparent insignificance in the scheme of things of sentience, and in particular of human sentience. Phenomenalism came to the rescue. I am sure that Ramsey accepted phenomenalism for intellectual, rather than emotional reasons, but it was a comforting doctrine none the less. He once wrote: 'My picture of the world is drawn in perspective, and not like a model to scale. The foreground is occupied by human beings, and the stars are all as small as threepenny bits. *I don't really believe in astronomy except as a complicated description of human and possibly animal sensation.*'* It is easy to see how this way of thinking helps, spuriously, to tame the vast astronomical spaces. Even extra-galactic nebulae are only actual and possible sense experiences! And yet, quite apart from the logical difficulties that I have raised against phenomenalism, it does seem to me quite unbelievable that atoms, stars, and nebulae should be mere fictions for ordering sense experiences, that the course of our sense experiences should be merely *as if* atoms, stars, and nebulae existed. Or to put it in a less question-begging way, the rather incoherent stream of our sense impressions is readily understood if they are thought of as due to our interaction with an objectively existing physical world, but on the phenomenalist theory it is a huge accident that they hang together in the way that they do. (Price and Ayer even go so far as to consider a possible world in which sense experience had a eurythmic rather than a 'physical object' type of order.) When we consider the scattered and gappy series of our sense experiences we should surely feel that this is surprising on the phenomenalist view, whereas it is just what we should expect on the realist view.

What are sense impressions, anyway? Modern philosophers have tended to use the technical term 'sense datum' where I have been content to talk, perhaps less precisely, in terms of 'sense im-

* *Foundations of Mathematics* (Routledge and Kegan Paul, London, 1931), p. 291 (my italics). I have made this passage part of the subject of an article 'Man's Place in the Universe', *Humanist*, March 1959. I have since found that Bertrand Russell quoted the same passage, with similar intent, in his book *My Philosophical Development* (Allen and Unwin, London, 1959), p. 130.

pressions' and 'sense experiences'. The notion of sense datum has in fact to be explained in terms of physical objects: to say that I am having a tomato-ish sense datum is to say no more than that it looks to me as though there is a tomato before my eyes. Why is it that phenomenalists do not take tomatoes and trees as uncontroversial? Why is it that they wish to analyse tomatoes and trees in terms of sense data? Part of the reason is what Ryle has, I think, called 'the bedrock assumption'. The idea is that we can reasonably assert corrigible propositions about tomatoes and trees only if we do so on the basis of incorrigible assertions about something else. It is sense datum statements which provide the incorrigible bedrock. A man who, sincerely and knowing the correct meanings of the words he uses, utters a sense-datum sentence, or its equivalent, such as, for example, 'it seems to me that there is a dagger before my eyes', cannot be wrong, as can the man who sticks his neck out and says 'there is a dagger before my eyes'. (Neglecting some doubts about incorrigibility to be raised in Chapter V.) The sense datum philosopher takes seriously in this context the injunction to found his house upon rock. And yet there is no need to suppose that our common sense and scientific knowledge needs to be founded on any absolutely incorrigible or nearly incorrigible bedrock. To use a simile of Popper's, you can perfectly well found a house on a swamp if you drive in enough piles deep enough.* And if you want to make your house still more secure you can drive in more piles and drive them deeper. There is no need for an absolutely secure foundation, so long as it is secure enough for the time being.

Let us therefore free ourselves from the sense datum prison and remember that we are in active contact with the material world, even if never quite incorrigibly so. Let us look in biological fashion at the process of gaining knowledge. Men are physical objects of a complicated sort. They react to stimuli from the environment in characteristic ways: their behaviour is modified by what happens to them and they acquire new behaviour patterns. This learning process is dependent on information coming in to our sense organs in the form of light rays, sound waves, and so on. There is nothing mysterious about the acquisition of knowledge, and simple examples of it can be demonstrated in the ability of

* Cf. K. R. Popper, *The Logic of Scientific Discovery* (Hutchinson, London, 1959), p. 111.

certain artificial machines to learn from experience. Physicists are more easily tempted towards phenomenalism than are biologists. Once you think biologically about perception you think in terms of the abilities of animals to react to stimuli. It is then difficult to think of material things as requiring analysis into sense data. Indeed, the boot is on the other foot.

PHENOMENALISM ABOUT SUB-MICROSCOPIC OBJECTS

Let us take it, then, that it is material objects, not sense data, which are uncontroversial. In other words, material objects are not to be understood in terms of sense data, but sense data are to be understood in terms of material objects. How this is to be done is a topic for Chapter V. At present I wish to consider the question of whether we are to regard the sub-microscopic particles postulated in physical theory as part of the 'furniture of the world', or whether we have to regard such theoretical entities as in some sense fictions, convenient ways of organising our talk about tables and chairs, trees and stars. I shall try to uphold a realistic view of these theoretical entities, and will try to establish that the elementary particles of physics are just as respectable entities as tables and galvanometers. By 'just as respectable' here I mean '*philosophically* just as respectable'. Unicorns are philosophically just as respectable as cows: it is for the zoologist, not the philosopher, to decide that there are no unicorns. Similarly, the physicist may come to replace his present theory of elementary particles with some other theory of what goes on at the sub-atomic level. Nevertheless, he will presumably postulate some new set of theoretical entities to replace the old ones. It is not for the philosopher to decide between one physical theory and another any more than it is up to him to become a zoologist and decide for or against the existence of unicorns. My problem is concerned with the ontological status of the physicist's theoretical entities, whatever they are.

The most extreme form of the view which I wish to oppose is that sentences about electrons, protons, and the like can be *translated* into sentences about galvanometers, cloud chambers, and the like. On this view electrons and protons are logical constructions out of macroscopic objects, just as the average man is a logical construction out of men. (We say that A's are logical construction out of B's when sentences containing the word for A's can be translated into sentences which do not contain this word, but which contain the word for the B's. In general, and as is not the case when A's can be explicitly defined in terms of B's, the new sentences will differ in other respects than the mere substitution of one expression for another. For example, the sentence 'The average man is 5 feet 6 inches tall' just means 'The sum of the heights in feet of all the men divided by the number of men is five and a half'.) However, it is now generally agreed among philosophers of science that no such explicit translation of theoretical sentences into observational ones is possible. In the first place, a theory in science has to say more than the empirical facts and generalisations which it is designed to explain. If it did not 'say more' it would be precisely equivalent to these facts and generalisations, and could not be used to predict any further facts and generalisations. For these further facts and generalisations could not be logically implied by the old ones. (If they did they would not be further facts: that Jones is a man is not a further fact beyond the fact that he is a bachelor.) A further difficulty has been pointed out by F. P. Ramsey* and R. B. Braithwaite.† Suppose that a new sort of experimental or observational fact, not predicted by a theory T, is discovered. It is natural to try to extend the theory T, by adding on new postulates in such a way that the theory now also predicts the new facts. Ramsey and Braithwaite have shown that if the theoretical terms of the theory are logical constructions of our observational ones (even though these last are universal generalisations), then it is not possible to modify T in the above way. This would mean that we could not extend our theories in the light of new evidence, but would have to construct radically new theories all the time.

I wish now to consider a theorem in mathematical logic which is sometimes held to show that theoretical terms are not needed in science. (Though I think that any theory constructed in accordance with this theorem would be very much open to objections on the lines of Ramsey and Braithwaite. But I shall also show other reasons why this theorem does not really show that theoretical terms are in any important sense eliminable in science.) The

* Essay on 'Theories', in *The Foundations of Mathematics, op. cit.*
† R. B. Braithwaite, *Scientific Explanation* (Cambridge University Press, 1953), Chapter 3.

theorem in question is due to William Craig.* Craig himself is extremely cautious about claiming philosophical importance of this sort for his theorem. There can, of course, be little doubt of the importance of his elegant theorem as a contribution to mathematical logic. In discussing Craig's theorem I shall have to refer to some technicalities of mathematical logic, and readers will lose little if they prefer to skip this small part of the present chapter. The next few pages are addressed to those who may think that Craig's theorem is a serious objection to the anti-phenomenalist thesis of this chapter.

Craig's theorem concerns a wide class of formal systems. It is sufficient here to say that any likely formalisation of a non-trivial physical theory would fall within this class. A formal system is a system of sentences for which there are quite definite rules of construction: *i.e.* we can always tell, in a routine way, whether any given sentence is well constructed or not. Actual languages, including the language of science, are, of course, not formalised. Arguments are not rigorous in the mathematical logician's sense, nor are they often rigorous in the slightly laxer sense of the pure mathematician. Nor are there strict formation rules in actual science. Is the sentence 'there is a life force in a lettuce' a meaningless (ill-constructed) sentence or is it just a false one? It is rather arbitrary how we answer such a question.

Let us suppose, however, that the language of some physical theory has been formalised with rigorous formation and transformation rules. Let T be this language and let S be a sub-language of T. That is, the vocabulary of S is more restricted than is the vocabulary of the more inclusive language T. Craig has proved that all the theorems of T which are expressible solely in terms of the vocabulary of S are also theorems of a language T' (axiomatised theory) which contains only the vocabulary of S. For example, to take the sort of case which interests us in this chapter, suppose that T is a theory containing observational terms such as 'cloud chamber' and also non-observational terms such as 'electron'. Then we can form, according to Craig's methods, a theory T' which contains no non-observational theorems of T. As far as observational consequences are concerned, T' is as comprehensive

* William Craig, 'On Axiomatisability within a System', *Journal of Symbolic Logic*, Vol. 18, 1953, pp. 30–2, and 'Replacement of Auxiliary Expressions', *Philosophical Review*, Vol. 65, 1956, pp. 38–55.

as T, and it could therefore be argued that non-observational terms such as 'electron' are dispensable, and that theories containing such terms are merely notationally handy equivalents for theories which do not contain them.

However, on second thoughts it may become apparent that Craig's theorem does not have this consequence for the philosophy of science. In the first place very few physical (or other) theories have been at all rigorously formalised. A good deal has been done, as by Sugar, Suppes, and McKinsey,* towards the axiomatisation of classical particle mechanics, but the rigorous axiomatisation of such a theory as quantum mechanics is an almost infinitely distant goal. Furthermore, in a rapidly developing subject, such as modern physics, any axiomatisation would become out of date almost overnight, and in any case if it were actually used, and were not a mere museum piece, it would have a fossilising effect on physical theory.† But the most important consideration is as follows.

The theory T' corresponding to the original theory T can be obtained by Craig's methods only if we proceed in a rather artificial way. Though in T' we do not need to talk about electrons, protons, and the like, we do need to talk about the *linguistic expressions* in T which correspond to the words 'electron', 'proton', etc. These linguistic expressions are, roughly speaking, classes of similar macroscopic objects, namely ink marks on paper. And it would seem to be an advantage if we could replace talk about dubious theoretical entities by talk about classes of macroscopic objects. Nevertheless, the procedure has an air of artificiality about it which becomes more evident when we consider that the theory T' would be a very odd-looking one. Let us consider the nature of the theory T'.

T' will be a theory with an infinite number of axioms. There is nothing in itself objectionable about this. For example, in a system of propositional logic we might specify that anything of the

* J. C. C. McKinsey, A. C. Sugar, and P. Suppes, 'Axiomatic Foundations of Particle Mechanics', *Journal of Rational Mechanics and Analysis*, Vol. 2, 1953, pp. 253-77. This is still not a complete axiomatisation in the sense required for Craig's theorem to apply, since it is done on the basis of an intuitive set theory.

† I have argued to this effect in my paper 'Theory Construction' in *Logic and Language*, Second Series, edited by Antony Flew (Blackwell, Oxford, 1953).

form 'If A then A or B' is an axiom. Thus, one of the infinity of axioms specified by this stipulation is 'If $2 + 2 = 4$ then $2 + 2 = 4$ or $7 + 5 = 12$'. So long as there is a routine process for deciding whether or not a given expression is an axiom, there is no reason why a set of axioms should not be infinite. (An example of an infinite set of true sentences which could not be a set of axioms is the set of all truths of arithmetic. There is no routine, or 'effective', process whereby we can decide whether or not a given sentence expresses a truth of arithmetic. All arithmetic is not, like long division, reducible to an algorithm.) With Craig's infinite set of axioms there is indeed an effective process for deciding whether or not a sentence belongs to the set. So there is no objection to be made on this score. Nevertheless, for a set of axioms for a branch of science, such as physics, there are other conditions which must be fulfilled. We require that the set of axioms be *simpler* and *more perspicuous* than the set of theorems to be proved. Now even granting the vagueness and obscurity of these notions of simplicity and perspicuity, it is pretty clearly the case that these notions are not satisfied in the case of the theory T'.

There is a way of assigning integers to linguistic expressions in a formal theory. This is known as Gödel numbering. Suppose $\alpha, \beta, \gamma, \delta$, constitute the alphabet of our theory. Let us assign numbers $3, 5, 7, 9$, say, to $\alpha, \beta, \gamma, \delta$ respectively. Then the sequence of expressions $\beta\alpha\gamma\gamma\delta$, say, would be represented by the number $2^5 . 3^3 . 5^7 . 7^7 . 11^9$. The number is the product of the first prime number raised to the power of the number assigned to the first symbol and of the second prime number raised to the power of the number assigned to the second symbol and . . . (and so on). We can also assign Gödel numbers to sequences of sequences of expressions, such as constitute a proof. Given a Gödel number, we can (since a number always factorises uniquely into primes) deduce the original linguistic expression or sequence of expressions. Now Craig's system of axioms is specified as follows: if A is an observational theorem which can be proved in T, then we have as an axiom of T' the formula A & A & A . . . & A with n A's, n being the Gödel number of the sequence of expressions which constitutes a proof of A in the system T. If n is not the Gödel number of a proof of A in T, then A & A & A . . . & A (with n A's) is not an axiom of T'.

There is certainly an effective process for deciding whether or not a given formula is an axiom of T'. We first check whether it is a conjunction of the form A & A & A ... & A. We count the number of A's. We check whether n is a Gödel number at all. (For example, A itself cannot be an axiom because 1 is not a Gödel number.) If n is a Gödel number we check whether it is the Gödel number of a proof of A in T. We then check whether it is a valid proof. It is important to grasp the fact that there is this routine method for deciding whether A & A & A ... & A with n A's is an axiom or not, under the conditions given for n. For some readers will say: 'Why not just specify that A itself is an axiom of T' if and only if it is a theorem of T?' This would indeed be trivial, if it could be done, but it cannot be done, for there is no routine method of telling whether a sentence A is a theorem of T.

Craig's set of axioms is, then, in one sense, a perfectly respectable one. But note the artificiality of the method as a device for producing postulates for a physical theory. We need to know the system T before we can construct T'. And if T is just a lot of ink marks, and is not capable of an objective interpretation, it does seem too much of an unbelievable coincidence that T' should work at all. It is beyond my powers of credulity to believe that the observational statements predicted by the theory T' should be just those which were to be expected on the basis of the theory T, unless there really were the entities putatively mentioned by expressions in T. The fact that in constructing T' we do not need to mention the entities mentioned in T but only their names does not remove the feeling that there would have to be an infinite number of coincidences if T were not capable of interpretation and objectively true. We may conclude, therefore, that Craig's theorem, important though it may be for the theory of axiomatisability in logic, is not a weapon which can be turned against philosophical realism about theoretical entities in science.*

'But what on earth do the words "objectively true" which you

* The significance of Craig's theorem for the philosophy of science is also discussed by C. G. Hempel, in his article 'The Theoretician's Dilemma', *Minnesota Studies in the Philosophy of Science*, Vol. 2 (University of Minnesota Press, Minneapolis, 1958), especially pp. 76–9. See also Grover Maxwell, 'The Ontological Status of Theoretical Entities', in H. Feigl and G. Maxwell (eds.), *Minnesota Studies in the Philosophy of Science*, Vol. III (University of Minnesota Press, 1962), especially pp. 17–19.

used in the last paragraph mean?' someone may object. 'What indeed does "real" mean? What do you mean by saying that electrons are *real*, not mere theoretical *fictions*?' Here a type of uneasiness manifests itself, which was well expressed by Bernard Mayo in an article some years ago in *Penguin Science News*.* I certainly do not mean merely that statements about electrons are not translatable into statements about observable things. As we saw, Ramsey and Braithwaite would agree to this, and yet from my point of view they still hold to an essentially phenomenalist position. Someone might hold that nation statements are not translatable into citizen statements. Yet he would probably still hold that in some sense nations are nothing 'over and above' citizens. And someone might hold that though statements about electrons are not translatable into macroscopic terms, nevertheless electrons are still, in a looser sense, theoretical fictions. But what can this sense be? Mayo tries to clarify the questions 'Do electrons exist?' and 'Are electrons real?' by comparing them to similar questions in ordinary life, when there is no doubt what we mean when we use the words 'exist' and 'real'. He rightly suggests that we can gain insight into the meaning of an assertion if we consider what the assertion is meant to deny. Now if I say that the table in front of me exists I am naturally taken to be denying that I am having an hallucination of a table or dreaming of a table. And, as Mayo says, those philosophers who assert that electrons exist are not trying to deny simply that they are hallucinatory or dream objects. They are trying to say something more than this. Compare also the sentence 'Electrons are real'. Often, as Mayo points out, when we say that something (a diamond, say) is real we are denying that it is an imitation or a sham one. We are obviously not wanting to say something of this sort about electrons. What, then, according to Mayo, could be meant by saying that electrons are real? Not much. According to him, to say that electrons are real is simply to say that the concept of the electrons occurs in a well-established theory.† This, as Mayo sees, puts electrons on a par with lines of force, for example.‡ The status of the concept of 'electron', on this view, is the same as that of 'line of force'. It occurs in a well-tested theory.

* B. Mayo, 'The Existence of Theoretical Entities', *Penguin Science News* No. 32, May 1954, pp. 7–18.
† *Ibid.*, p. 17.   ‡ *Ibid.*, p. 16.

Now I wish to say that lines of force, unlike electrons, *are* theoretical fictions. I wish to say that this table is composed of electrons, etc., just as this wall is composed of bricks. Of course, the electrons, etc., are spatially scattered in a way in which the bricks are not. In this respect a swarm of bees would be a better analogy than a wall of bricks. On the other hand, nothing is composed of lines of force. The concept of a line of electric force is a useful theoretical fiction: it provides a useful picture to help us discuss the distribution and directions of the forces that would be exerted on unit electric charge at all places within a certain region of space. That there is something artificial about it can be seen from the fact that 2π lines of force leave a unit charge, and so the number of lines of force in a certain region depends on our arbitrary choice of the unit of electric charge.* Electrons are a different kettle of fish from lines of force.

Of course, some physicists may feel uneasy about the distinction that I have made. For (as I have discovered) they may feel that lines of force are *not* fictional: that (according to the conceptions of *classical* physics, in which the notion of lines of force has its habitat) a line of force is a very real state of the surrounding ether, and indeed an electric charge is no more than a point at which these lines of force meet together. If one imagines an infinity of lines of force leaving a charge one gets near to a picture of the objective state of the surrounding ether. This nevertheless leaves untouched the contention that the notion of lines of force so defined that 2π of them leave a unit charge is an artificial and fictitious one. Even if we take a non-arbitrary unit of electric charge, say the charge on an electron, there is still the logical impossibility that there could be exactly 2π lines of force emerging, from it. (There cannot be exactly 2π of anything, whether sausages immaterial souls, or lines in space!) And I wish to assert that electrons, unlike lines of force in the sense just defined, are concrete entities.

Suppose someone says that electrons are theoretical fictions whereas tables and grains of sand are concrete entities. Then this is what I deny when I say that electrons are real. When I say that a diamond is real I am, as Mayo points out, denying that it has the sort of defectiveness that a sham or artificial diamond has. When I say that electrons are real I am admittedly not denying that

---

* I owe this observation to Mr B. D. Ellis.

they are defective in any way. But I am, I think, saying something of this sort, not about electrons, but about the *concept* of the electron. The sort of contrast I am concerned to make when I say that electrons are real is the contrast with such things as lines of force. This explains why Mayo is right, in a way, in saying that the question of whether electrons are real is not one that naturally arises. But it does arise in the context in which we are interested in the sort of defectiveness that concepts can have, which is that of being fictional, for example. When we say that elves are not real we are saying something about the way in which the word 'elf' is used—a pretence, or fairy story, way. The word 'real' stands alone here, not followed by a noun as in 'These are real diamonds'. (Though we can keep the same sense provided we use a very general, empty, noun such as 'thing'.) If, on the contrary, we said that 'elves are not real men' we would suggest something quite different: not that 'elf' is a fairy-story word, a word used in pretence assertions, but that elves are in some way artificial or imitation men. This is not what we mean when we say simply 'elves are not real'.

My suggestion is, then, that 'X's are not real', as opposed to 'X's are not real Y's', can indeed be taken as asserting a sort of defectiveness or shortcoming, but a defectiveness or shortcoming of the *concept* of an X, not of the X's themselves. In which case the question 'Are electrons real?' may perhaps have a clear meaning, though not the same sort of meaning as has 'Are these real diamonds?' When someone says that 'electrons are real' he is denying that 'electrons are not real'. By the latter it is not meant that electrons are defective, imitation, or counterfeit: if electrons are not real, then there are not any to be defective, imitation, or counterfeit. But nor is he denying the reality of electrons in the way in which a man who wishes simply to deny the usefulness of the electron theory might say that electrons are not real. The man I am thinking of is not denying that electrons in a sense exist, but he is saying that their existence is to be understood solely in terms of macroscopic concepts. This would be to assert a sort of defectiveness in the concept of the electron (or perhaps of the word 'electron'). It would be to say that electrons are theoretical fictions like lines of force, not even *non*-existent objects like unicorns. On his view, electrons neither do nor do not exist in the sense in which mountains or unicorns do or would exist. It could, however, even be said that 'Unicorns are not real' itself asserts a sort of defectiveness, not of unicorns again, but of the concept of a unicorn, namely that the concept of a unicorn does not apply to anything. This is a different sort of defectiveness of a concept from that which I am suggesting that the concept of an electron might or might not have.

A man who says that electrons are theoretical fictions is saying that they do not occur in the series: stars, planets, mountains, houses, tables, grains of wood, microscopic crystals, microbes.* This is a series of concrete objects, ranging from the large to the small. No one is likely to deny that a powder of copper sulphate is made up of microscopic crystals just as a wall is made up of bricks. But he may feel resistance to saying that crystals are made up, in the same obvious sense, of atoms. What is the source of this resistance? I ask this question because I think that the resistance is something which should be overcome.

We must distinguish two senses in which a man might deny that a crystal is made of atoms (or ultimately electrons, protons, etc.) just as a wall is made of bricks. The first and less important sense is that he might be denying the theory of atoms, electrons, protons, etc. It is most unlikely, of course, but he might have, or claim to have, revolutionary experimental evidence which showed that our present-day physical conceptions are untenable. The issue between such a man and an orthodox physicist is one which gives rise to no philosophical trouble. It is a dispute to be settled in the ways in which scientific disputes normally are settled. On the other hand, a man who denied that crystals were made up of atoms in the way in which a wall is made up of bricks might be agreeing with the usual scientific views about atoms, but might be trying to make the point that they are unlike bricks in being theoretical fictions. Why does he want to say that atoms are theoretical fictions, though he does not want to say this of the particles of a fine powder which are visible only under the microscope? What is the basis of his confidence about the particles of the fine powder? Indeed, as Grover Maxwell has pointed out, a man who disbelieved that *molecules* were real things, but allowed that crystals (of sugar, say) were real things, would have to face the difficulty that accord-

* See Max Born, 'Physical Reality', *Philosophical Quarterly*, Vol. 3, 1953, pp. 139–50, especially p. 141.

ing to modern valency theory a crystal is in an important sense a single huge molecule.*

Suppose that a person looks through a very low-power microscope. He sees a lump of sugar, say, looking twice as large. He does not need to know the theory of the microscope to know that what he sees is a lump of sugar. It looks just like a lump of sugar, only bigger. Even a savage who knew nothing of optics would tend to say that what he saw was a lump of sugar. Compare the way children say 'car' when they see a picture of a car, even though they have been taught the word 'car' in relation to actual cars. No doubt they do this even before they have any conception of what a picture is: certainly they do it before they learn the *word* 'picture'.

In this sort of way we get to think that a microscope shows us what things would look like to us if they were many times bigger or if we were many times smaller. We thus think of the minute crystals of the powder as only contingently invisible to our naked vision. If we were much smaller we should see them as plainly as at present we see bricks and motor cars.

When we pass from what we see with the ordinary microscope to what we see with the ultra-microscope, and still more when we pass to what we see with the electron microscope, a different situation presents itself. In such a case we could not expect our savage to interpret what he sees: here a knowledge of optics or electron optics is essential. Nevertheless, given this knowledge, we can see that it is still a contingent fact that we cannot see with the naked eye what we can see with the ultra-microscope or the electron microscope. For example, if there were as many electron beams through space as there are at present photon beams, and if we had eyes constructed on the electron microscope principle, and if our biological structures were capable of standing up to the intense radiation to which they would be subjected, then we might be as much at home in the world of individual living cells, and even of macromolecules, as we are at present in the world of cats and dogs. (Except in so far as the mere fact of the vast *number* of the minute entities might cause us to get lost.)

It is no more than a contingent fact that we cannot see such things as bacteria and protein molecules. Can we go further and

---

* Grover Maxwell, 'The Ontological Status of Theoretical Entities', in H. Feigl and G. Maxwell (eds.), *Minnesota Studies in the Philosophy of Science*, Vol. III (University of Minnesota Press, 1962).

say that it is just a contingent fact that we cannot see individual atoms, or even protons and electrons? Theoretical considerations prevent us from taking this further step. In any ordinary sense of the word 'see' what we see must have a definite position, and our seeing of it must leave it substantially unaffected. These conditions could not hold with the fundamental particles. It is important to remember that the word 'electron' gets its meaning from the part it plays in physical theory. Physical theory rules out the possibility of our seeing electrons and the like. It is therefore not a merely contingent fact, but something built into the meaning of the words 'electron', etc., that the fundamental particles cannot be seen. In the case of a photon it is peculiarly obvious that however microscopic was our vision we could not see one. Photons explain seeing, and therefore could not be seen. For would one see a photon by means of a further photon? Indeed, as I think I once heard Professor Herbert Dingle wittily remark, if photons could be seen we could not see anything else: they would get in the way of whatever we wanted to see!

One can readily admit, then, that there are theoretical reasons why however small we were we could not see the theoretical entities of physics. In this respect these entities *do* differ from bricks, microscopic crystals, and bacteria, and even perhaps from protein molecules. But is this a good reason for putting them into a different *ontological* category? The mere fact that there are theoretical reasons why they cannot be seen gives no ground for saying that they are in any sense fictions. Theory asserts the existence of the elementary particles and *also* explains their nonvisibility. Surely we need not fall back to Berkeley and suppose that *esse* is *percipi*.

Of course, it is true that the elementary particles are rather queer things. It is also true that if the present physical theories are given up or radically modified we may have to give up asserting the existence of these particles. Not that this is as solid an objection as might appear at first sight. There is no reason to suppose that 'electron' will ever suffer the fate of 'phlogiston'. Whatever it is that we describe, or possibly misdescribe, in the old language will have to be described, or misdescribed, in the new language. When de Broglie began to talk of the electron as a wave packet, then 'wave packet' still tried to describe what 'particle' did before. The situation is not all that different from the case of the sea serpents which later mariners described as schools of porpoises: there is something which is described or misdescribed by both the ancient and modern sailors.

But if it be granted that we *need not* fall back into phenomenalism it may be replied that there is nevertheless no reason why we *should not*. I wish to argue, on the contrary, that there is a most telling theoretical reason why we should not adopt a phenomenalist interpretation. I shall also point out that there is also a reason why as a matter of *practical policy* it would be unwise to be satisfied by such a phenomenalism. Let us take the former reason first.

If the phenomenalist about theoretical entities is correct we must believe in a *cosmic coincidence*. That is, if this is so, statements about electrons, etc., are of only instrumental value: they simply enable us to predict phenomena on the level of galvanometers and cloud chambers. They do nothing to remove the *surprising character* of these phenomena. Admittedly the physicist will not be surprised in the sense that he will find these phenomena arising in unexpected ways: his theory will have instrumental value in preventing this sort of surprise. But, if he is reflective, he ought still to find it surprising that the world should be such as to contain these odd and ontologically disconnected phenomena: *i.e.* the phenomena are connected only by means of a purely instrumental theory. Is it not odd that the phenomena of the world should be such as to make a purely instrumental theory true? On the other hand, if we interpret a theory in a realist way, then we have no need for such a cosmic coincidence: it is not surprising that galvanometers and cloud chambers behave in the sort of way they do, for if there really are electrons, etc., this is just what we should expect. A lot of surprising facts no longer seem surprising. Marshall Spector has in correspondence drawn my attention to the importance for the problem of the reality of theoretical entities of C. S. Peirce's notion of 'abduction'. (We argue from A to B by abduction when we point out that the previously surprising fact A is no longer surprising on the assumption of the truth of B.)

On theoretical grounds, then, we should regard phenomenalism as both unproven and unplausible. There are also good practical grounds for taking this point of view. If we are phenomenalists we shall become dangerously complacent about the present state of physics. If we are phenomenalists why *shouldn't* we treat an electron as a wave on Mondays, Wednesdays, and Fridays and as a particle on Tuesdays, Thursdays, and Saturdays? Why should we seek for a unitary hypothesis? In the history of science, as P. K. Feyerabend has shown, a positivistic attitude has frequently been inimical to progress. Positivism would once have supported the Ptolemaic theory against the Copernican one, by showing that at the time it was the better prediction dodge of the two. It supported phenomenological thermodynamics and resisted the kinetic theory of gases. And today it opposes, *a priori*, any attempts to construct alternatives to the prevailing Copenhagen interpretation of quantum mechanics. It is easy to see that positivism is easily allied with dogmatism. The received theories in physics, however inelegant and unsatisfactory in various respects, must obviously be good prediction dodges as far as they go. Hence a physicist who adopts an instrumentalist position will be satisfied with the prevailing point of view, and will strongly resist any attempt to produce alternatives. Indeed, his dogmatic attitude may even prevent him from describing correctly the observations which would refute his theories. This is because observation in physics is always theory-laden, and not just a matter of making pointer readings and the like.*

It is important, however, that we should take account of the real physical difficulties in a realistic interpretation of modern physics. In particular, we should not content ourselves with too simple an idea of the entities whose real existence we are postulating. It is an unfortunate fact that historically the proponents of the Copenhagen interpretation of quantum mechanics have used very questionable positivistic arguments, and have often talked as though their position rested on a verification theory of meaning. To which a philosopher may be tempted to object: 'I agree

* On these and other points see the following papers by P. K. Feyerabend: (1) 'Realism and Instrumentalism' in M. Bunge (ed.) *The Critical Approach, Essays in Honor of Karl Popper* (The Free Press, New York, 1964); (2) 'Problems of Microphysics', in R. G. Colodny (ed.) *Frontiers of Science and Philosophy* (University of Pittsburgh Press, 1962). (3) 'Das Problem der Existenz theoretischer Entitäten', *Probleme der Wissenschaften, Festschrift für Victor Kraft* (Vienna, 1960), pp. 35–72; (4) 'How to Be a Good Empiricist', B. Baumrin (ed.) *Philosophy of Science, The Delaware Seminar,* Vol 2 (Interscience, New York, 1963), pp. 3–39. (5) 'An Attempt at a Realistic Interpretation of Experience', *Proceedings of the Aristotelian Society,* Vol. 58, 1957–58, pp. 143–70 (6) 'Niels Bohr's Interpretation of the Quantum Theory', in H. Feigl and G. Maxwell (eds.) *Current Issues in the Philosophy of Science* (Holt, Rinehart and Winston, New York, 1961), pp. 371–89.

that for physical reasons we cannot simultaneously *measure* the position and momentum of an electron. Nevertheless, this is not to say that it *has not* a simultaneous position and momentum. We are unable to ascertain what it is, but we may meaningfully talk of it.' Even such good writers as Landé and Popper have tried to assimilate the uncertainty of the position of an electron to the uncertainties we get in such games as bagatelle.

Unless the real difficulties in quantum mechanics can be dealt with, the philosophical objections to the Copenhagen interpretation, which consist only in exposing the positivistic preconceptions thereof, will be found unsatisfactory by physicists. As Feyerabend has pointed out, purely philosophical arguments will be felt by physicists to be unsatisfactory, since there are good *physical* reasons for refusing to admit a precise position and momentum to the elementary particles. I shall concentrate on the well-known two-slit experiment, the importance of which in this connection has been stressed both by Feyerabend and by A. Grünbaum.

When de Broglie introduced the conception of the electron as a wave packet he thought of it as a wave packet in some underlying medium, much as a wave packet in the theory of sound would be a localised but travelling region of compressions and distensions of air. Later developments in the quantum theory led to the necessity of a different interpretation of the wave function. According to this interpretation, the function does not determine the wavy state of some substratum but rather the probability of finding the electron in a certain place. The values of the probability, that is, are distributed according to the same type of mathematical equation as are the values of the height of a wave. This interpretation would seem to restore the conception of the electron as a particle rather than a wave. But there is further trouble both for the particle interpretation and for the wave interpretation. This can best be explained by the well-known text-book example of the electron which passes through a diaphragm in which there are two adjacent slits.*

In the diagram (Fig. 1) a stream of electrons is ejected from the point *S*. They pass the diaphragm *D* through two slits *A* and *B*.

---

* On the crucial importance of this sort of example, see A. Grünbaum, 'Complementarity in Quantum Mechanics and its Philosophical Generalisation', *Journal of Philosophy*, Vol. 54, 1957, pp. 713–27.

It should be said that for theoretical simplicity the experiment is a rather idealised one: in actual practice the slits *A* and *B* would correspond to the spaces between adjacent planes of a crystal. The diagram is not drawn to scale, and *A* and *B* must be thought of as very close together. There is some method of detecting where the electrons strike the screen *T*. We can suppose that this method is a very sensitive one, so that we can detect the arrival of only a single electron at the screen *T*. There is nothing technically impossible about this. Let us first take the case where very many electrons are being shot out from *S*. Thinking of electrons purely as particles, we should expect to find them hitting the screen *T* at the points *A'* and *B'* where the straight lines *SA* and *SB* meet the screen. This is not so, however. What is found is that at some points on *T*, in particular mid-way between *A'* and *B'*, many electrons strike, whereas at others none strike. There is a pattern of interference bands, similar to those which one gets in the optical experiments which demonstrate the wave nature of light. This suggests that what is being emitted from *S* is radiation in the form of waves. When the waves reach *A* and *B* they are diffracted

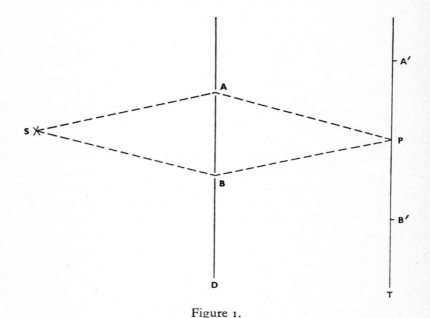

Figure 1.

from A and B as though A and B were their sources. Suppose that they strike the screen at P. If the paths SAP and SBP differ in length by an even number of half wavelengths the two beams reinforce, and if they differ by an odd number of half wavelengths they cancel out. Hence the interference bands.

We seem constrained, therefore, to suppose that not particles but waves are being emitted from S. But then we are brought up against a fact which prevents us from taking this interpretation of the situation. If we reduce the intensity of the radiation from S we shall ultimately reach the stage where at any one time only one point on T is found to be hit. It is once more as though we were dealing with particles. A particle hits T at one particular place. In time, of course, various places on T will have come to have been hit by many particles: the regions on T where many and no particles respectively hit the screen are given by the interference bands which occur when a whole stream of electrons is shot out from S. It appears that a single electron may hit T at all sorts of different places, though it is more probable that it will hit at some places than at others. Do we go back to thinking of the electron as a particle, then? No, because how would that explain the interference bands? Moreover, consider what happens if we leave slit A open and close B. The single electron will not reach the screen at a point such as P, but will go instead approximately to A'. When both slits are open the electron presumably, if it is a particle, must go through A or B. But whichever it does, for it to reach P it is essential that the *other* slit be open. This is most odd, and it makes it hard for us to conceive of the electron as a particle, *i.e.* as an entity precisely located in space. Yet if it is a wave why is it that all of it strikes the screen at P, say: why is it that there is not an interference pattern over a region of the screen, though of course a weaker one than when intense radiation is emitted from S?

The upshot would appear to be that the electron is not localised in space in any visualisable way. For reasons already given, I do not wish to fall back on a phenomenalistic evasion of the dilemma. But the above remarks do show that any realistic philosophy of the theoretical entities must not be too naïve. It must reckon with the very real difficulties in giving a non-phenomenalist interpretation of physics. (It is perhaps an intellectual value judgment that these difficulties are likely to be outweighed by the intrinsic implausibility of the phenomenalistic attitude, as well as the practical dangers thereof.) After all, it is very unlikely that quantum mechanics is in its final form, and it may be drastically revised, with some of its fundamental assumptions altered. (The final clause of the last sentence indicates the irrelevance to the present issue of Von Neumann's proof, which, so it is often claimed, proves the essentially indeterministic character of quantum mechanics.*) One way out of the dilemma may lie in the development of deterministic theories of microphysics on the lines foreshadowed by such writers as D. Bohm and J.-P. Vigier. Another way of re-solving the apparent paradox of the motion of the particle in the two-slit experiment (does it go through one slit, both slits, or neither?) may lie in suggestions which have recently been can-vassed, that space and time are statistically significant only: that position may be a property appropriate only on the macroscopic level. Banesh Hoffman, in a popular book, *The Strange Story of the Quantum*,† has made such a suggestion and has brought it to bear on the puzzle about wave-particle dualism. He says (*ibid.*, p. 197):

> 'If space and time are not the fundamental stuff of the universe but mere particular average, statistical effects of crowds of more fundamental entities lying deeper down, it is no longer strange that these fundamental entities, when imagined as existing in space and time, should exhibit such ill-matched properties as those of wave and particle. There may, after all, be some innate logic in the paradoxes of quantum physics.'

There are indeed various indications in the physical literature that the concepts of space and time may be essentially macroscopic. Recently E. J. Zimmerman has written an interest-ing survey of the subject in an article in the *American Journal of Physics* (1962).‡ He suggests that space and time are not concepts which can be applied to the microentities of physics. There are properties which these microentities have, such as charge, isotopic spin, mass, and strangeness, and it is in terms of such concepts that physical theory will develop. The micro-entities, Zimmerman says, will 'interact in ways that must also be described abstractly, that is, without reference to space and

---

* See Feyerabend, paper (2) cited in footnote to page 40.

† Dover, New York, 1959, pp. 197–8.

‡ E. J. Zimmerman, 'The Macroscopic Nature of Space–Time', *American Journal of Physics*, Vol. 30, 1962, pp. 97–105. This article contains various useful references to the literature.

time'. The interaction of a vast number of such microentities results in the creation of a space–time framework: the concepts of space and time are concepts which apply on the macroscopic level only, much as temperature has meaning on the macroscopic level but not for single particles, or for small numbers of particles. (Elementary particles, so conceived, remind one of the non-spatial and non-temporal Kantian 'things in themselves'.)

Zimmerman bases his suggestion on researches by Salecker and Wigner. He formulates his position in too operationalist a way for my taste, but it may be that this formulation is inessential. What these researches claim to show is that within a microscopic system it is impossible to measure distances or periods of time with a precision which goes anywhere near even that permitted by the uncertainty principle. Of course, these suggestions about the essentially macroscopic nature of space and time remain mere suggestions only, and they are important here mainly as a possibility which is of philosophical interest. Certainly no viable physical theory has yet been developed in accordance with this suggestion.

Philosophers may object that the suggestion can be refuted *a priori*. How can we think except with reference to a space–time framework? Now ordinary or common-sense thought clearly must work within a space–time framework, but this is not surprising, since ordinary or common-sense thought is concerned only with macroscopic objects. It may be said that Zimmerman, as quoted above, used the word 'interact', and must not an interaction be in time? To this verbalistic reply we suggest that the objector choose a word signifying a relation of interdependence which does not necessarily imply spatio-temporal interdependence. It may be asked how a billiard ball, which has position, can be made up of a cloud of entities which have not positions themselves. We have already seen that the concept of temperature provides a counter-example to this objection. Here is another. The eighteenth-century physicist Boscovitch had a theory according to which the world was made up of point masses surrounded by spheres of attraction and repulsion. Let us consider a world made up of such point masses. Clearly the point masses themselves have no shape, but the things which are made up of them have: there might be a spherical or cubical cloud of point masses, rather like a spherical or cubical swarm of bees. The ultimate particles, the point masses, themselves have no shape, but on the macroscopic level we can talk of shape perfectly meaningfully. (I have taken Boscovitch's hypothesis for my example because of its simplicity and clarity, but what I say applies to modern physics too, because though the modern elementary particles are not quite like point masses, they are equally unlike billiard balls.) Can we not suppose something analogous to this in the case of spatial position, too: that the elementary particles of modern physics do not have position, but that, in some way which is at present unclear to us, they give rise to position as a statistical property on the macroscopic level? Perhaps some uneasiness may be felt on the ground that the analogy between shape as a statistical property in Boscovitch's theory may not be analogous to the present notion of position as a statistical property on the macro-level. This may arise because in a sense we think we can visualise point masses, whereas how can we visualise positionless entities? The answer is that we cannot visualise even Boscovitch's particles: we pretend to ourselves that we can do so by visualising *very small* volumes. It is impossible to visualise positionless particles, but this is not to say that we cannot give sense to such a notion within the framework of a theory. After all, philosophers in the past have talked of positionless entities, such as God and immaterial souls, or even olfactory sense-data, without *obviously* talking nonsense.

The above suggestions have been produced largely as a piece of mind-broadening: to suggest that it is unlikely that microphysics is now in its final state, and that surprising new developments may overcome the difficulties of 'wave or particle?' But whatever the result, there are weighty reasons against giving up lightly a realistic view of the entities postulated by physical theory: we can remain philosophical realists even if we admit that they are very queer entities indeed. I do not wish it to be thought that my philosophical point of view stands or falls by whether any of the above very speculative suggestions turns out to be valid. Such a suggestion might indeed make it *easier* to accept a realistic view. But you can be a realist about electrons without holding that they are particles, or anything like particles. Certainly classical ideas about these entities have had to be drastically revised, and no doubt our present ideas will undergo great changes in future. In fact, this seems inevitable: modern quantum mechanics is in such an inelegant mess, and the number of 'ultimate' particles is getting so large, that a new and simpler theory must surely be waiting to be discovered. The great and compelling reason for refusing to regard the elementary particles as theoretical fictions (such as lines of force, for example) is that unless something like what quantum mechanics tells us is true of some underlying reality, then that the macroscopic laws are what they are seems to be too much of a coincidence to be believed. Suppose that a detective finds a lot of footprints, bloodstains, and so on. If the criminal were a theoretical fiction for relating footprints and bloodstains hitherto found to one another, then it would seem too good to be true that it should actually issue in true predictions of further footprints and bloodstains and even of missing five-pound notes. But if there really were a criminal, then these predictions would no longer be surprising.

Indeed, I would wish to go further than merely to defend the physicist's picture of the world as an ontologically respectable one. I would wish to urge that the physicist's language gives us a *truer* picture of the world than does the language of ordinary common sense. Of course, I do not mean by this that most of the statements we make in ordinary life are not *true*. If I say that the tea cup is on the table I can surely be saying something true. And even when I say that the table is 'solid' I may be understood as saying something true: that the table has not got holes in it through which things can be pushed, as is the case with a sieve or a colander. Up to a point, Susan Stebbing's strictures against Eddington were perfectly justified.* But Stebbing went too far. There is also a perfectly good sense in which it is true and illuminating to say that the table is *not* solid. The atoms which compose the table are like the solar system in being mostly empty space. (This was Eddington's point.) So though most common-sense propositions in ordinary life are true, I still wish to say that science gives us a 'truer picture' of the world. In Chapter IV I shall be concerned with one important way in which ordinary language tends to give us a false picture of the world: this arises because of our concepts of colour and other so-called 'secondary qualities'. But in this chapter I have had rather different fish to fry. After criticising phenomenalism about macroscopic objects I

---

* L. S. Stebbing, *Philosophy and the Physicists* (Methuen, London, 1937), pp. 54 ff.

have gone on to discuss the modern tendency to oppose phenomenalism about tables and chairs but to be phenomenalist about
electrons and protons. Recent philosophers have unfortunately
tended to give an ontological priority to everyday concepts and to
have 'a sharply . . . definite view of the world: a world of solid
and manageable objects, without hidden recesses, each visibly
functioning in its own appropriate pattern'.* They have been
wedded to the concepts of common sense every bit as much as the
medieval pre-Galilean philosophers were, but they have been less
open about it.

In the same way, proponents of the Copenhagen interpretation
of microphysics have been wedded to *classical* physics. They argue
that since this is the physics of macroscopic instruments whereby
we interpret our observations, this must remain stable whatever
the advances in microphysics. That this is not so can be shown
(as by Feyerabend)† by posing one simple question: why *classical*
physics? Why not, for example, Aristotelian physics, or even
witchcraft, which was once just 'scientific common sense'?
Similarly, we must reject the view that there are laws at the
phenomenological or macro-level which are sacrosanct, and
which the micro-theories explain. We must insist, as Sellars and
Feyerabend have done, that the micro-theories can directly explain observations, such as of the outcome of the two-slit experiment. A particularly flagrant example of the disposition to regard
phenomenological theories as sacrosanct is given by E. A. Milne.
In his *Modern Cosmology and the Christian Idea of God*,‡ he discusses
the second law of thermodynamics and its relation to the question
of the 'heat death' of the universe. He refuses to adopt the point of
view of statistical thermodynamics, and rests his argument entirely on phenomenological thermodynamics. He says (p. 147):
'The data are macroscopic; the conclusion is macroscopic. Hence
it ought to be possible, avoiding all statistical treatments of
thermodynamics, to pass directly from the factual basis to the con-

* The quotation is from the last paragraph of S. Hampshire's critical notice
of Ryle's *Concept of Mind*, *Mind*, Vol. 59, 1950, pp. 237–55. I do not think,
however, that a phenomenalist doctrine about theoretical entities is in fact
implied by Ryle's theses in *The Concept of Mind*. The quotation from Hampshire, however, beautifully hits off a certain attitude of mind which I wish to
oppose.

† See footnote to page 40.

‡ Clarendon Press, Oxford, 1952. See Chapter 10.

clusion.' It is clear that he regards statistical thermodynamics as an adjunct to phenomenological thermodynamics—to be linked to phenomenological thermodynamics by means of 'correspondence rules' and to be rejected if it conflicts with the phenomenological theory. On the contrary, we must reject this account of the relation between the two theories. Statistical thermodynamics does not need to be linked to macrophysics by means of so-called 'correspondence rules'. Indeed, not only *need* it not: it *must* not be so linked. For phenomenological thermodynamics is simply *false*. (In saying this I am much influenced by Feyerabend.) After all, such a phenomenon as the Brownian motion *refutes* phenomenological thermodynamics. What is needed is not that the micro-theory should explain a macro-theory or macro-laws to which it is linked by correspondence rules. What is needed is, as Wilfrid Sellars* and Feyerabend† have pointed out, that it should explain why observable things obey, to the extent that they do, those macro-laws. Thus, for example, statistical thermodynamics explains why things obey the laws of phenomenological thermodynamics to the extent that they do obey the laws of phenomenological thermodynamics. The moral for quantum mechanics is obvious. We may indeed use some of classical physics for the theory of parts of our measuring instruments when there is no reason to believe that such theory would differ from the full-scale (and impossibly difficult) quantum mechanical treatment. But with this proviso, part of the object of quantum mechanics is to explain why macro-entities obey, to the extent that they do, the laws of classical physics. (This is the 'correspondence principle' in physics which as thus construed is sensible, and not to be confused with the modern philosophic notion of 'correspondence rules', which is objectionable.)

* Wilfrid Sellars, 'The Language of Theories', in H. Feigl and G. Maxwell (eds.), *Current Issues in the Philosophy of Science* (Holt, Rinehart and Winston, New York, 1961), pp. 57–77.

† Comments on Sellars' 'Language of Theories', *ibid.*, pp. 82–3.

III

PHYSICS AND BIOLOGY

IN order to prepare the way for later chapters I need to say something about the relationship between the physical and biological sciences. This will be particularly important in our concern with the mind–body problem. Both biologists and philosophers have frequently wondered why biology does not seem to have the precision and the close-knit theories which we find in physics and chemistry. Sometimes they hope that in future biology will be brought into such a precise and unified form. Partly for this reason J. H. Woodger has tried to axiomatise genetics.* However, there has been a very odd look about such attempts to treat a biological discipline on the model of a close-knit physical theory. I shall wish to argue that there are no biological theories, in this sense, and that there are not even biological laws. (Though there are biological *generalisations*.) *A fortiori* there are no *emergent* biological laws, as has been supposed by some philosophers. By an emergent law I mean one which relates to some complex entity, but which is in principle inexplicable in terms of the simple entities. It is important for me to deny the existence of such emergent laws, since it is a central thesis of this book that animals and men are very complicated mechanisms.

It has sometimes been thought that even at the level of chemistry there are emergent laws. It has been said, for example, that however much we knew of the properties of sodium and of

* J. H. Woodger, *The Axiomatic Method in Genetics* (Cambridge University Press, 1937).

chlorine, we could never predict the properties of salt (sodium chloride). This analogy has frequently been used to make plausible the existence of emergent laws and properties of life and of mind. The analogy is, however, based on an error. In fact, it is in principle possible to deduce the chemical properties of salt from the purely physical properties of sodium and chlorine respectively. From the purely spectroscopic properties of these substances we can, through the quantum theory of the chemical bond, deduce the way in which sodium will combine with chlorine and, in principle at least, how it will react with some other compound whose chemical properties will be deduced from the spectroscopic properties of the elements making it up. (I say 'in principle' simply because valency theory is very complex, and it may not be practicable to carry out the calculations I have in mind except in simple cases. But equally it is not possible to predict the position of Jupiter indefinitely far in the future: the complexities of the perturbations from other planets may defeat us. But this is not to say that the planets do not follow Newton's or Einstein's laws.) It is therefore just false that chemical laws are emergent and in principle inexplicable in terms of physical ones. Notice, moreover, that the relevant physical properties that I have mentioned have been spectroscopic ones. There has been none of the circularity that would have been involved if I had taken as a physical property that of combining with chlorine to form a compound with such and such chemical properties. In theory, though doubtless not in practice, physicists might have discovered the chemical bonds of sodium and chlorine from purely physical facts about them and without having met with any chemical compounds containing sodium or chlorine.*

Of course we could easily imagine that physics would never have been able to explain the chemical bond. As it is, however, the example of chemical combination does not support the idea of emergence. Of course, there is a *trivial* sense in which new qualities emerge when simples are put together to form a complex. In the last chapter we saw that while Boscovitch's point masses

---

* On this point see C. W. Berenda, 'On Emergence and Prediction', *Journal of Philosophy*, Vol. 50, 1953, pp. 269–74. An extended discussion of the notion of emergence is given by E. Nagel in Chapter 6, Section 4, of his book *The Structure of Science* (Harcourt Brace and World, Inc., New York and Burlingame, 1961).

do not possess shape, a cloud of them could. Even four point masses have (in general) the property of determining a tetrahedron, but it would be absurd to say that each one of them determined a tetrahedron. Thus, even on a purely mechanistic theory there are properties possessed by complexes which are not possessed by their elements. The theory of emergence, if it is to say anything interesting, clearly must assert emergence in some sense other than this trivial one.

Consider a device such as a wireless receiver. It contains a lot of components, such as condensers, coils, resistances, valves, and transformers. If these are connected up in the right way we have a wireless receiver: if they are connected up haphazardly or not at all we do not have a wireless receiver but a junk heap. If you like to say that the ability to receive wireless signals of a certain wavelength is an emergent property you can. Nevertheless, it is certainly a property which could have been foreseen by a sufficiently knowledgeable physicist who knew the wiring diagram and who had never seen or heard of the components being arranged together as a wireless set. The property of being able to receive wireless signals is certainly not an emergent property in the non-trivial sense, namely a property which could be discovered only by observation of the complex apparatus as a whole.

Not only do I deny the existence of emergent laws and properties, but I even deny that in biology and psychology there are laws in the strict sense at all. There are, of course, empirical generalisations. There are not any biological laws for the very same reason that there are not any laws of engineering. Writers who have tried to axiomatise biological and psychological theories seem to me to be barking up the same gum tree as would a man who tried to produce the first, second, and third laws of electronics, or of bridge building. We are not puzzled that there are no laws of electronics or of bridge building, though we recognise that the electronic engineer or bridge designer must use laws, namely laws of physics. The writers who have tried to axiomatise biology or psychology have wrongly thought of biology or psychology as a science of much the same logical character as physics, just as chemistry is. I shall try to show that the important analogy is not between biology and the physical sciences but between biology and the technologies, such as electronics. At once, however, I must forestall a possible misconception. In drawing an analogy between biology and electronics I do not intend to suggest that biology is an applied science. It is in the logical structure of their explanations that I wish to draw the analogy between biology and electronics, and so the analogy will hold, if it holds at all, even when we are considering the most practically useless parts of biology. I do not, of course, deny that much of biology is pursued primarily on account of intellectual satisfaction, not on account of its applications. It is in quite a different respect that I shall find the analogy between biology and electronics.

Physics and chemistry have their *laws*. For example, there are the laws of motion in classical mechanics, the laws of electrodynamics, and the equations of quantum mechanics. In chemistry there are the innumerable laws expressed by chemical equations. There is one very important feature of these laws. These laws are universal in that it is supposed that they apply everywhere in space and time, and they can be expressed in perfectly general terms without making use of proper names or of tacit reference to proper names. Such laws I call 'laws in the strict sense'.

Biology, it seems to me, does not contain any laws in the strict sense. Even Mendel's laws, it will turn out, are generalisations rather than laws in the strict sense. First of all, let us consider a proposition that is obviously one of natural history. Consider the proposition that albinotic mice always breed true.* What are mice? They are a particular sort of terrestrial animal united by certain kinship relations. They are defined as mice by their place in the evolutionary tree. (In this sense of the word 'mouse', a so-called 'marsupial mouse' is not, of course, a mouse.) The word 'mouse' therefore carries implicit reference to our particular planet, Earth. Alternatively we might point, or refer by some appropriate linguistic description, to a member of the species, and say that animals which have the appropriate kinship relations to this one are to count as mice. Provided we make use of this proper name 'Earth' or some uniquely referring expression or gesture in the definition of 'mouse', then our law that albinotic mice always breed true is perfectly general. It cannot be falsified by any biological facts about denizens of planets of remote stars, because no creatures there, however mouse-like, would be mice in the required sense. But though in the logician's sense it is general, and though it is very likely true, the proposition 'albinotic mice always

* Cf., for example, H. Kalmus, *Genetics* (Pelican, London, 1948), p. 58.

breed true' is not a law in the strict sense. It carries with it implicit reference to a particular entity, the planet Earth.

Could we not, however, define 'mouse' in a different way? Suppose that there is a certain set of properties A_1, A_2, ... A_n possessed by all mice, and on this planet only by mice. Thus, A_1 might be the property of being four-legged or of being very closely related to a four-legged animal. (This last clause is put in so as to take care of possible freak mice with three or five legs.) No doubt we could find a set of properties such that, so far as terrestrial animals are concerned, all and only mice possessed them. The trouble is that now we have no reason to suppose our law to be true. The proposition that everything which possesses the properties A_1, A_2, ... A_n and which is albinotic also breeds true is very likely a false one. It may be that the universe is infinitely big, in which case, to make use of a remark of F. Hoyle's,* somewhere in the depths of space there must be a cricket team to beat the Australians. Indeed, if we accept the premiss that there is a non-zero probability of a sufficiently large region of space (*e.g.* a sphere 100 light years in diameter) containing a cricket team to beat the Australians, then it follows at once that in an infinite universe there must be an infinite number of such teams. But leaving such pleasant fantasies to one side, the universe, even if it is finite, is nevertheless very big indeed, and on some planet belonging to a remote star there may well be a species of animals with the properties A_1, A_2, ... A_n and of being albinotic but *without* the property of breeding true. Or consider such general propositions of biology as those describing the process of cell division. If 'cell' is defined in relation to *terrestrial* organisms, then these propositions about cell division are not laws in the strict sense. If 'cell' is defined without explicit or implicit reference to the planet Earth, then we have no reason to suppose that these propositions are true. Is it not very likely that in planets of remote stars there are cells which divide according to rather different methods?

My conclusion so far is that if the propositions of biology are made universal in scope, then such laws are very likely not universally true. If they are not falsified by some queer species or phenomenon on earth they are very likely falsified elsewhere in the universe. The laws of physics, by contrast, seem to be truly

* F. Hoyle, *The Nature of the Universe* (Blackwell, Oxford, 1950), p. 95.

universal. Why is there this difference? Part of the answer seems to be this. The physicist, and to a lesser degree the chemist, talks about things which are relatively *simple* or else *homogeneous*. Thus, classical particle mechanics deals with point masses. Rigid mechanics can be developed by integration from particle mechanics. For example, it can be shown that a homogeneous sphere behaves gravitationally like a point mass at its centre. In rigid mechanics we do not need to take account of the admittedly very complex minute structure of any actual rigid body. The physical properties of the atom are explained because the theory of the atom can be reduced to that of simpler particles, such as electrons, protons, and neutrons. It is important that such small simple constituents are believed to be ubiquitous in the universe. In this respect electrons and protons are not like albinotic mice, or even diploid cells or, for that matter, chromosomes.

What about macroscopic laws, such as the gas laws and the laws of thermodynamics? These arise on account of statistical averaging, and once more depend on homogeneity and the un-importance of fine structure. The physicist can treat a gas as a homogeneous thing in a way in which the biologist or the en-gineer cannot treat a cell or a radar installation. There are, I would submit, no laws in the strict sense about organisms, because organisms are vastly complicated and idiosyncratic structures. No one expects even all motor cars of a certain make and year to behave exactly alike. Yet a motor car is a very simple structure compared with even a single living cell. Still less, therefore, should we expect to find laws, as opposed to generalisations, about organ-isms. Even if such generalisations should turn out to have few exceptions in our terrestrial experience, it would be rash in the extreme to suppose that they have universal validity in the cosmos. A generalisation of biology is thus even unlike those laws of physics which are only approximately true, such as Boyle's law and Newton's law of gravitation. Boyle's law is very nearly true except when the pressure of a gas is high, and Newton's law is very nearly correct except in the vicinity of some very massive body. That is, we can specify the circumstances in which such a law breaks down, and we can specify the limits of accuracy within which it may be expected to hold. With these reservations and within these limits such a law is as applicable to the farthest nebula as it is to our own neighbourhood. Consider, by contrast, such an apparently fundamental law as that of Mendelian segregation. Even terrestrial populations do not segregate quite in accordance with the Mendelian principle, for a multitude of reasons, of which the chief is the phenomenon of crossing over. Even if we tried to protect our law by adding clauses such as 'if there is no crossing over', we should be pretty sure to be caught out by some queer method of reproduction obtaining on other spheres. Of course, there may well be good reasons why life on other worlds must be expected to have a rather similar chemical constitution to life on ours. Perhaps in every case we may expect it to have begun with the creation of amino-acids and the combination of these into larger molecules. Nevertheless, it would be altogether too specu-lative to assert that things have always gone on in other planets as they have done here, and that, for example, the genetic codes are necessarily embodied in nucleic acid molecules as is the case here. Perhaps so, perhaps not. In any case, we are here talking at the biochemical level. Some philosophers, impressed by the neatness and simplicity of the Mendelian laws, may conceive of genetics as a possible 'universal science', analogous to physics. I have already indicated, however, that in genetics the situation is not so simple, and indeed genetics can be understood in its full complexity only if it is approached from the cytological point of view. And here we are back at 'engineering'.

An analogy may help to bring out the implausibility of the supposition that in biology there could be laws in the strict sense. Consider a certain make of radio set. Can we expect to find univer-sal truths about its behaviour? Surely we cannot. In general, it may be true that if you turn the left-hand knob you get a squeak from the loudspeaker and that if you turn the right-hand knob you get a howl. But of course in some sets this will not be so: a blocking condenser may have broken down or a connection may have become loose. It may even be that the wires to our two knobs may have been interchanged by mistake in the factory, so that with some sets it is the left-hand knob that produces a howl and the right-hand knob that produces a squeak. If there are no universal truths about all radio sets of a certain make and pattern, still less are there laws about, say, *all superheterodynes*. Of course there may be some universal properties which are true by defini-tion, such as that all superheterodynes contain a frequency changer. But this, of course, tells us nothing, and certainly does not ensure that the particular piece of hardware before us, with 'superheterodyne' written on it, in fact contains a frequency changer. A mistake may have been made in the factory, and by some extraordinary fluke it may be working on some other principle.

From a logical point of view biology is related to physics and chemistry in the way in which radio-engineering is related to the theory of electromagnetism, etc. Biology is not related to the physical sciences in the way in which, for example, the theory of gravitation is related to the kinetic theory of gases. That is, biology is not a theory of the same logical sort as physics though with a different subject matter. Just as the radio-engineer uses physics to explain why a circuit with a certain wiring diagram behaves as it does, so the biologist uses physics and chemistry to explain why organisms or parts of organisms (*e.g.* cell nuclei), with a certain natural-history description, behave as they do. A very large, if not preponderant, part of biology consists in these natural-history descriptions. We must not think of natural history as being merely about such things as lions and tigers, gum trees and bamboos. It is also about nucleoli, mitochondria, and other such small entities. The description of these small entities is logically on a par with generalisations about lions and tigers, and is not like a law of nature. Descriptive biology consists in generalisations of natural history, not laws in the strict sense. So while, roughly speaking, radio-engineering is physics plus wiring diagrams, biology is physics and chemistry plus natural history.

On this view, biology is ultimately biochemistry and biophysics. Of course, some biological explanations fall short of this ideal. We may explain a phenomenon as due to some hormone, even though we have very little idea of the chemical structure of this hormone. Again, a great deal was done with the notion of the gene, even before it was discovered that a gene is probably a nucleic acid molecule. Even now not a great deal is known of the chemistry of such molecules. To pursue the analogy with radio-engineering, in many parts of biology we have got down to a 'block-diagram' but have as yet no knowledge of the detailed wiring diagram. Our explanations are therefore partial and tentative.

If it is asked whether biology can be made an exact science the answer is 'No more and no less than technology'. If by an 'exact science' is meant one with strict laws and unitary theories of its

E   57

own, then the search for an exact biological science is a wild-goose chase. We do not have laws and theories of electronics or chemical engineering, and engineers do not worry about the lack. They see that their subjects get scientific exactness from the application of the sciences of physics and chemistry. No one wishes to axiomatise electronics. Why should Woodger have wished to axiomatise genetics? There are no real laws of biology for the very same reason that there are no special 'laws of engineering'.

This conclusion is, I think, borne out by the different ways in which mathematical statistics may enter into theories. The fact that biologists use statistical methods, and therefore some fairly sophisticated mathematics, may make us suppose that biology has its unitary and special theories just as physics has. In biology we frequently have to decide whether an experimental result is significant. Let us take a crude example. Suppose that we put some mineral into the soil and we find that we get bigger cabbages than we did before. Is this due to what was put into the soil? After all, the cabbages are going to vary in size, to some extent, anyway, and it may be merely by chance that we have got a bigger lot on this occasion. Statistics may enable us to calculate the probability of our bigger cabbages having turned up purely by chance, and if this probability is small we may become fairly confident that the new mineral helps to make bigger cabbages. In genetics such reasonings as to the likelihood or otherwise of accidental factors producing the experimental results can be very subtle and intricate. Mathematical statistics helps the biologist to get at the reality which is masked by chance variations. Let us call this the 'extra-theoretical' use of statistics.

The mathematical statistics which occurs in physics can be very intricate and subtle too. Consider the dynamical theory of gases. Here, however, the statistical reasonings have a different function. They are not used here in order to estimate the significance of experimental results, to pull aside the curtain of chance variations. They are used in order to explain how a multitude of randomly varying microscopic events can average out so that we get definite macroscopic laws. Thus, the use of statistics in gas theory (and various other branches of physics) is different from its characteristic use in biology, and this ties up with my characterisation of biology as a science without laws of its own in the strict sense. Let us call this second type of use of mathematical statistics which we find in gas theory the 'intra-theoretical' use of statistics.

Certain qualifications to the last paragraph now have to be made. I do not wish to deny that in physics, often enough, statistics is used in the sense of the theory of errors, that is, in the extra-theoretical way. Contrariwise, in the theory of evolution we have studies of the spreading of genes in populations which constitute an intra-theoretical use of statistics. Similarly, in ecology we find an intra-theoretical use of statistics. It is significant, however, that the theory of evolution and ecology are not, in the logician's sense, typically 'scientific' in nature. They are quite obviously 'historical' subjects. They are concerned with a particular and very important strand of terrestrial history. No doubt there are analogous histories on remote planets, but in the theory of evolution we are concerned with the hereditary relationships of terrestrial creatures only, and so we are not concerned with laws in the strict sense. If we try to produce laws in the strict sense which describe evolutionary processes anywhere and anywhen it would seem that we can do so only by turning our propositions into mere tautologies. We can say that even in the great nebula in Andromeda the 'fittest' will survive, but this is to say nothing, for 'fittest' has to be defined in terms of 'survival'. If the theory of evolution is concerned with terrestrial history it is even more obvious that ecology is too.

Let us return to the extra-theoretical use of statistics in the physical sciences. It is perhaps significant that if we think of the theory of errors as applied to the physical sciences the first thing which is likely to come into our heads is astronomy. Now astronomy is very much a history rather than a science analogous to physics. It is concerned very largely with the explanation of the particular facts of the planets, stars, and nebulae. However, this point should not be pressed too far, because we can think of the stars not as particular objects of historical interest but as huge laboratories for the testing of physical laws. Similarly, the planets have acted as test bodies for the validation of Newtonian dynamics. In such cases astronomy becomes a part of physics rather than an application of it: in these cases we are interested in the particular facts because they test our theories. (In the other type of case we are interested in the physical theories only because they explain the particular historical facts about the heavenly bodies.)

The distinction between the historical discipline of astronomy and the science of physics would become even more blurred if physics should turn out to have a cosmological basis (as is to some extent the case with the general theory of relativity), for in this case physics would itself be historical in nature. But even then there would still be a vast difference between physics and what we are accustomed to regard as natural history.

I have tried to argue, then, that those parts of biology which use intra-theoretical statistics are those that are most obviously historical in nature, and so the comparison with physical theories such as the dynamical theory of gases must be a superficial one. I have also tried to argue that extra-theoretical statistics occur characteristically in those physical sciences which are most historical in nature. My conclusion is that the occurrence of sophisticated mathematics in biology does not refute my general diagnosis, which is that biology is not a science which stands to physics and chemistry in the sort of way in which these stand to one another. We should not expect to find 'biological theories' but rather the application of physics and chemistry to the explanation of generalisations of natural history.

Someone may feel puzzled at this stage. It looks as though I have drawn a line through nature, and yet the difference between an atom, a molecule, a gene, a cell, and an animal seems to lie only in increasing complexity of physical structure. The answer is that the line I have drawn is a methodological one rather than an ontological one. The difference is that between using propositions of observable fact in order to test laws and using laws in order to test propositions of observable fact. Thus, in physics we may look to see if there is an electric charge inside a closed conductor, and by this test the inverse square law of electrostatic attraction stands or falls. (If, and only if, the inverse square law is true will there be no charge inside a closed conductor, however much the outside of the conductor is charged up.) In the days when the experiment was a 'live' one the physicist was more sure of his observations than of the inverse square law. In biology, on the other hand, we are more sure of the laws we use (the laws of physics and chemistry) than we are of the observational facts, the 'wiring diagram'. Clearly there must be fields of investigation in which we are equally unsure of the relevant laws and of the observational facts, the 'initial conditions' or the 'wiring diagram'. Here our distinction will become blurred. Moreover, I must now slightly qualify my previous classification of chemistry with physics. Consider a chemist who studies the structure of a protein molecule by means of X-rays. Here he can be more sure of the basic chemical laws that determine the structure than he is of the structure itself. It is the structure, therefore, that he sets out to determine by means of his experiments, and his study of protein molecules takes on much of the logical character that I have been attributing to biology. Conversely, if viruses of a certain sort should turn out to be a certain sort of macromolecule whose formula could be ascertained, then the theory of such viruses might become a branch of chemistry. (The practical difficulties in the way of such an eventuality are, of course, colossal. If a virus is a macromolecule, or small complex of macromolecules, it is almost certainly too complex for theory to be able to make much of it. The computations needed would be enormous. Moreover, the macromolecules might be capable of being squashed, twisted, or bent, in which case the laws of their functioning would not depend on the chemical formula alone.) There is not a sharp division in nature between the objects of physical type science and those of biological type science: the difference is one of methodology. In the former type of science we are interested in laws, whereas in the latter type of science we are interested in the natural history of structure and in the explanation of why things with this structure behave as they do. Compare the application of physics to wiring diagrams in the case of electronic engineering.

However, though there is not a sharp division in nature between the objects of the physical sciences and those of the biological sciences, there is, of course, a non-sharp division, which is one of complexity of structure. The methodological division does reflect this non-sharp division in reality.*

PSYCHOLOGY

The ideas of this chapter can be applied also to psychology. Psychology is indeed itself a biological science. Its progress has

* My views would therefore appear to be very much in harmony with those of Joseph Needham, in his book *Order and Life* (Cambridge University Press, 1936). On the difference between biological generalisations and laws of nature see W. I. Matson's solution to *Analysis* Problem No. 12, *Analysis*, Vol. 18, 1957-58, pp. 98-9.

been slowed by wrong ideas about methodology, more so than with biology generally. This is perhaps because psychologists have been unsure of themselves and have therefore been influenced in their methodology by logic text-book ideas about the nature of science. Psychologists have tended to search for strict laws of the stimulus-response type, and to integrate these laws in a body of what may be called 'molar' theorising: that is the theories concern the animal as a whole. This conception of psychology has been very well criticised by B. A. Farrell in an address 'On the Limits of Experimental Psychology'.* Farrell is concerned, as I am, with psychology as a pure science. There is, of course, much else which comes under the purview of psychology and for which other methods are appropriate: for example, psychometrics, social psychology, industrial psychology. Farrell has argued persuasively that the failure of the usual theories in psychology is due to the fact that they are at the molar level. One should not expect to find strict laws of the stimulus-response sort, though one may find useful generalisations. And if one is to hope for any important explanatory successes one must get down to the neuronal level or even below it: that is, one must have testable hypotheses about the structure and working of the animal's nervous system. Or, failing this, one must at least conjecture something on the lines of a radio-engineer's 'block diagram'. A good example of the right way to set about psychology is the following. Suppose that you do experiments on octopuses, as in the interesting work of N. S. Sutherland.† You find that they react differentially to vertical and horizontal rectangles, for example, but that they do not react differentially to rectangles at different oblique angles. You then try to guess the sort of

* B. A. Farrell, 'On the Limits of Experimental Psychology', *British Journal of Psychology*, Vol. 46, 1955, pp. 165–77. A defence of psychology as a biological science has been given by D. O. Hebb, though with salutary warnings. See his paper 'Alice in Wonderland, or Psychology among the Biological Sciences', in H. F. Harlow and C. N. Woolsey (eds.), *Biological and Biochemical Bases of Behaviour* (University of Wisconsin Press, Madison, 1958), pp. 451–67.

† N. S. Sutherland, 'Visual Discrimination of Orientation and Shape by the Octopus', *Nature*, Vol. 179, 1957, pp. 11–13. (Also letter commenting on this by P. C. Dodwell, *ibid.*, p. 1088. Letter by Sutherland in reply, *ibid.*, p. 1310.) A pioneering and instructive paper on shape recognition is J. A. Deutsch, 'A Theory of Shape Recognition', *British Journal of Psychology*, Vol. 46, 1955, pp. 30–7. See also J. A. Deutsch, *The Structural Basis of Behaviour* (Cambridge University Press, 1960), Chapter 11.

neuronal hook-up which would account for this behaviour. You try to test this hypothesis by trying further experiments on the visual discriminations of octopuses, accepting, of course, any hints provided by the anatomy of their nervous system. It is good policy to begin with simple nervous systems such as those of octopuses: one day, when we fully understand octopuses and other similar creatures, we may aspire to understand more advanced animals and even men rather better than we do at present. There seems to me no reason why not only perceptual abilities but all other abilities, and other traits of interest to psychologists, should not eventually be studied in this way. Moreover, until this sort of thing happens psychology will lag behind the other biological sciences and will be no more than a body of empirical generalisations and of practical techniques.

IV

THE SECONDARY QUALITIES

IN the previous chapter I have given a physicalist interpretation of biology and psychology. That is, I have argued that these sciences, in so far as they are anything more than a body of empirical generalisations and practical techniques, are an application of physics and chemistry to natural history, much as electronics is an application of physics to wiring diagrams. It may be objected that as far as psychology is concerned we have left out something important. It may be felt that psychology must consist in something more than behaviouristics and neurophysiology, since otherwise it leaves out the facts of *consciousness*. A consideration of this objection will have to wait for Chapter V. But quite apart from this, it may be felt that our physicalist interpretation of science entails that science cannot encompass everything in the world. Colours are not vibrations in the ether, nor are sounds vibrations in the air. The world of physics is a colourless, soundless, odourless, and tasteless world. What about the blueness of the sky, the greenness of the grass, the fragrance of the clover, and the buzz of the bees?

It may be said, therefore, that the physicalist view of the world is an inadequate one, because it leaves out of account the so-called 'secondary qualities', of colour, sound, smell, and taste. It is this contention which I am concerned to rebut in this chapter. I shall contend that we are perfectly able to fit the secondary qualities into our picture. I shall analyse the secondary qualities in terms of the reactions of organisms (in particular, human beings) to stimuli, and I shall do this in a way which is perfectly compatible with the view of this book that organisms are simply very complicated physico-chemical mechanisms. In particular, there are two important philosophical views about the secondary qualities which I shall be concerned to refute.

There are indeed well-known considerations which show that the secondary qualities (*e.g.* colour) which we immediately perceive in sight, hearing, smell, and taste are not part of the world as described in the physical sciences. Suppose that you see a red tomato. What is it in the tomato that gives rise to the perception of redness? It is the state of its minute parts, the atoms on its surface, which is such that when sunlight falls on to the tomato preponderantly the longer wavelengths (in the visible spectrum) are reflected towards our eyes. The physicist does not need the word 'red': he can do what he wants simply by talking about the wavelengths of light. (Astronomers do indeed talk about 'red' and 'blue' stars, but their meaning could be conveyed by saying 'stars that radiate light of relatively long wavelengths' and 'stars that radiate light of relatively short wavelengths'.) Similarly, when you hear a note struck on the piano what is going on in the external world can be described by specifying the frequencies of vibrations in the piano wire and in the surrounding air. With smell it is the presence of certain molecules in the air which reaches our nostrils, and with taste there is a similar story to be told. The scientific description of the world makes no use of words for colour, sound, smell, and taste. Does this mean that the scientific description of the world is incomplete, and that there are properties which we sense in immediate experience, but which lie outside the purview of physical science?

There are two different types of view about the secondary qualities, which are nevertheless alike in that they place the secondary qualities outside any physicalist world picture. I shall be concerned to refute them both, and to put forward a theory of the secondary qualities which explains why scientists have no use for them, and yet how they can be understood within a physicalist world view. I shall concentrate mainly on *colour*, which is perhaps the most difficult to understand of the secondary qualities.

CRITICISMS OF TWO PHILOSOPHICAL VIEWS ABOUT COLOURS

The two types of view about the secondary qualities which I wish to refute I shall call the Objectivist view and the Subjectivist view respectively. I shall state these views in relation to colour: it will be obvious to the reader what the corresponding view of the other secondary qualities would be.

The first view I shall call the Objectivist view. It is very nearly that of naïve pre-Galilean man. According to it, colours are intrinsic qualities of physical objects. They need no elucidation in terms of the sense experiences or reactions of human beings: they are just properties of physical objects, with no essential relation to human or other percipients. The redness of a tomato, for example, goes along with a power to produce certain sense experiences in normal human percipients when the tomato is illuminated by sunlight, but on the Objectivist view the quality redness is one thing and the power is another thing.

The second view which I wish to oppose I shall call the Subjectivist view. This is essentially Locke's view. According to it, the colour redness in the tomato is not an intrinsic property of the tomato, but is the power the tomato has, when it is illuminated by the right sort of light, to produce red sense data in a normal human percipient. It is the sense datum which has the intrinsic and unanalysable property or *quale* redness. It should be noted that it is the power in the object, not the *quale* of the sense datum, which Locke calls the 'secondary quality' of redness. Unfortunately Berkeley and other later writers have used the expression 'secondary quality' to refer not to the power in the external object (indeed, for Berkeley there is in a sense no such external object), but to the *quale* of the 'idea' or sense datum.* I shall oppose the notion of redness as a *quale* of a sense datum, but it is well to point out the positive merits of Locke's position: his recognition that the redness of the tomato is a relational and partly anthropological property of things.

There is an oddity in the notion of colour as a *quale* of a sense datum. It is this: that we can never be sure that you see the same colours as I do. To use an illustration of John Wisdom's: suppose

* See the illuminating exegesis of Locke by Reginald Jackson in his article, 'Locke's Distinction between Primary and Secondary Qualities', *Mind*, Vol. 38, 1929, pp. 56–76.

you see the Union Jack as green, yellow, and purple while I see it as red, white, and blue. That is, when you see a proper Union Jack you get the same colour experiences as I get when I see a green, yellow, and purple one. Suppose also that the reverse holds, and that you see the green, yellow, and purple Union Jack as though it were a proper red, white, and blue one. (Let us indeed suppose that there is a one–one mapping of this sort which applies to all colours. Suppose, for example, colours arranged on a colour circle, at the centre of which will be white and on the circumference of which will be the spectral colours. Intermediate saturations (or 'whitenesses') will occur in positions between the centre and the circumference. Suppose that a colour S is mapped into a colour S' which is on the same diameter as S but an equal distance from the centre of the circle on the other side from S. According to this mapping, one colour and one colour only, white, will be mapped into itself, and so the reader can, if he wishes, replace my example of a green, yellow, and purple Union Jack by that of a green, *white*, and purple one.) The difference between you and me, on this assumption, will be an undetectable one, because, of course, I call the thing that produces red sense data in me 'red', while you call the thing that produces green sense data in you 'red'. For example, we both understand the traffic lights all right. The actual *qualia* of the sense data would seem not to matter at all so long as there is a one–one mapping of my *qualia* on to the *qualia* produced by the same stimuli in you.

The Objectivist might suppose that his view is open to no such oddity. For he will probably claim that the *qualia* of things are immediately apprehended by some sort of intuition, and so you and I can apprehend identically the same *quale*. This intuition is presumably something which supervenes when the causal perceptual process described by psychologists and physiologists occurs. If this is the Objectivist's story it is of an extreme scientific implausibility. It is certainly incompatible with the view of man as an extremely complicated physico-chemical mechanism. We might ask just where and how such a capacity for intuition supervenes in the evolutionary history of the animal kingdom. How could a change in the structure of a gene (which is a very large molecule) do anything but alter (through chemical influences) the *machinery* of the developed body? If the Objectivist does not admit that we have intuitions of these objective *qualia*, but says nevertheless that the *qualia* of bodies exist, though they are in fact different from the Lockean 'powers' of things to cause experiences (or perhaps differential reactions) in human beings, then for all we know the correlation between the *qualia* and the powers is not one–one. For all we know, the intrinsic *quale* of the tomato may be quite different from that of the post box.

I shall neglect, however, to press the above objections. For both the Objectivist and the Subjectivist views face sufficiently damaging considerations of another sort. These considerations turn upon the seeming impossibility of fitting these *qualia*, in any plausible way, into the body of our scientific knowledge. It looks today as though the ultimate laws of nature are those of physics. In the previous chapter I argued for a physicalist philosophy of the biological sciences. Now if there are *qualia*, then they cannot plausibly be fitted into this sort of scheme. Let us take the subjectivist view first. According to this view, there exist sense-data with specific *qualia*. These are presumably correlated with very complex neurophysiological goings on in the brain, but they must on no account be confused with these goings on. It would appear therefore that if there are such things as sense data with unanalysable *qualia*, then human psychology cannot be entirely fitted into a physicalist scheme. There would have to be special irreducible laws which relate the complex neurophysiological processes to the corresponding sense data. These laws would have to be isolated offshoots from the main network of scientific explanation: as H. Feigl has put it, these laws would be 'nomological danglers'.*
Such ultimate laws are hard to believe in, partly because such isolated 'danglers' seem uncharacteristic of the general development of our scientific knowledge, but also for a more specific reason. We expect ultimate laws of nature to relate simple entities. Such, at any rate, has been the whole tendency of science. Even Newtonian dynamics relates to hypothetical 'particles' in the first place, and is applied to reasonably homogeneous rigid bodies by the mathematical process of integration. Again, the second law of thermodynamics is a macroscopic law, but it is true in virtue of the statistical averaging out of microscopic goings on. Wherever we look in science we do not find anything analogous to the sort

* H. Feigl, 'The "Mental" and the "Physical"', *Minnesota Studies in the Philosophy of Science*, Vol. 2 (University of Minnesota Press, Minnesota, 1958), pp. 370–497, especially pp. 382 and 428.

of ultimate law which would have to be postulated by the Subjectivist. It would have to be an ultimate law which would relate something simple, a sense datum with an unanalysable *quale*, to a very complicated and non-homogeneous process involving millions of neurons (and hence countless millions of millions of ultimate particles) and depending on numerous negative feed-back mechanisms of complicated sorts. This does seem quite unbelievable, and we should surely try to find an alternative to any philosophical theory which has such a fantastic consequence.

In the same sort of way, the Objectivist also has to postulate some very queer ultimate laws. Philosophers often write as if there were a simple one–one correlation between a colour and the corresponding light radiation, but of course in most cases the light emanating from a body consists of a continuous spread of wavelengths of varying intensity over all or part of the visible spectrum. If we envisage such a mixture of wavelengths of light as being represented by a graph there is an infinite number of such graphs which correspond to a given colour. It is impossible therefore to think of the facts of colour vision as being given by a simple correlation between colour and wavelength. Therefore if there were colour *qualia* the laws relating the light-reflecting powers of surfaces to *qualia* would be far from simple. If we look further at the nature of colour vision we shall see that it is unlikely that there should be such laws. (We shall see in what way colour is an *anthropocentric* concept.)

The facts of colour vision are very complex, and they are still not well understood. Let us take colours equivalent to those of monochromatic light of wavelengths (say) 700 mμ, 540 mμ, and 390 mμ. (These are the wavelengths chosen in Chapter 3 of P. J. Bouma's *Physical Aspects of Colour*.* I refer the reader to this chapter of his book for the facts about the three-colour theory of vision which I am briefly summarising in this paragraph.) Call these colours R, G, and B. Then by additive mixing of suitable amounts of R, G, and B we can get beams of light which can produce most colour sensations. (Additive mixing can be done, for example, by directing the beams of light of the various colours on to a white screen. It must not be confused with subtractive mixing, which is the sort you get when you mix paints. Suitable amounts of R, G, and B additively mix together to give white. Subtractive mixing

* Philips Industries, Eindhoven, Netherlands, 1949.

69

would produce black.) There are exceptions to the rule that any colour can be got by a suitable mixture of R, G, and B. Thus, the pure spectral colours between B and G cannot be precisely got in this way. However, if you mix a certain proportion of R with such a spectral colour you get a colour which can be got by mixing B and G. We can express this fact by saying that the spectral colour can be got by a suitable proportion of B and G together with a negative proportion of R.

With this added complication the three-colour theory of vision works fairly well, and it has been speculated that there are three different sorts of light-sensitive substances in any cone of the retina, the substances being most sensitive to light in the regions of B, G, and R respectively. However, there are further complications in the facts of colour vision which cannot be explained by the three-colour theory. Suppose that we look at a certain object against a varied background. E. H. Land* has argued that if the light coming from the various parts of this background varies in the intensity of the various wavelengths in a fairly random way, then the seen colour of an object depends not so much on the actual wavelengths reflected from it as on the relative distribution of long and short wavelengths over the entire scene. Thus, by photographing a scene through two filters of different colours and projecting the two photographs on to a screen simultaneously from two projectors which have different filters, we can see colours corresponding to spectral wavelengths which may be even greater or less than the spectral wavelengths which roughly correspond to the colours of the filters. One can even in suitable circumstances get a full range of colours on the screen using just a red filter and a white filter. (One would expect simply various shades of pink.) In such cases the colours we see probably depend on complicated computations in the brain of the signals from the whole area of the retina, and the phenomena cannot be explained by the simple mechanism of the three-colour theory.

Land's results thus enormously strengthen the thesis that the colours seen by a normal percipient do not depend on any simple property of the object seen, but that they depend partly on the special peculiarities of the human visual apparatus (the eye and the visual areas of the brain). They make even more unplausible the view that what we see in colour vision corresponds to some in-

* *Scientific American*, Vol. 200, No. 5 (May 1959), pp. 84–99.

trinsic *quale* of the external object. If the *quale* had been correlated with something simple such as a particular wavelength of light, then the Objectivist theory would have been a little more plausible. We have seen, however, that the *quale* would have to be correlated with something very much more complicated which depends on the idiosyncracies of the human eye and nervous system. That this is so seems to be as unbelievable as astrology, which suffers from the same delusion that the characteristics of the universe tie in closely with the doings of human beings.

As we saw, the three-colour theory of vision is not quite satisfactory in that: (*a*) we have to bring in negative quantities of colour, and (*b*) it does not account for the surprising facts adduced by E. H. Land. But even if I weaken my case by admitting the adequacy of the three-colour theory, I can still bring out forcibly the anthropocentricity of our colour concepts. The human colour visual apparatus can, if the three-colour theory is true, be simulated by three photo-electric cells.* The three cells must be most sensitive for respectively three different wavelengths of light, and their maximum sensitivities will in general be different from one another. Within limits we can make an arbitrary choice of the wavelengths for which the cells are most sensitive, but having chosen these, we are not free to choose the relative maximum sensitivities of the cells. These must be experimentally determined and depend on the characteristics of the normal human visual apparatus. It would therefore be an infinitely unlikely occurrence that the combination of the three cells should correspond to something objective in nature, out of any relation to the human eye or arbitrary photo-electric device. In this way colour differs from temperature. There are good physical reasons why there should be a simple correlation between the expansion of mercury in a thermometer tube and something objective and non-arbitrary in nature, namely temperature defined thermodynamically. We could indeed say the same, with due cautions and reservations, for the human sense of hot and cold. We have seen, however, that what corresponds to the human visual sense, in the way in which the thermometer corresponds to the human temperature sense, is a rather arbitrary photoelectric arrangement.

It should now be apparent why anyone who is acquainted with the scientific facts ought to regard the Objectivist view of colours

* See Bouma, *op. cit.*, pp. 154–6.

as quite unplausible.* I should remind the reader that I could have pitched the case even stronger if I had considered the defects of the three-colour theory of vision. Even on the relatively simple three-colour theory the case is quite bad enough for the Objectivist. Moreover, if there are still any Objectivists left I ask them to envisage the inhabitants of some other planet for whom a five-colour theory of vision was appropriate. These creatures would have a visual apparatus corresponding to a combination of five photo-electric cells. The Objectivist may reply that we with our 'three-colour' apparatus see in a glass darkly what the extra-terrestrial creature with his 'five-colour' apparatus sees better. I then ask him to envisage creatures with 'eleven-colour' vision, 'nineteen-colour' vision, and so on until we get to a creature with 'infinite-colour' vision. This last being would be analogous to a physicist who plots a distribution curve of the intensity of the light radiated from a point on a surface against its wavelength. Such a being would indeed attain to something objective in nature, but not something which is simple or like colours as we know them.

We may conclude, therefore, that the Objectivist theory is at least as scientifically unplausible as we saw the Subjectivist theory was. It is therefore important that we should search for some tenable account of colours which does not make mention of *qualia* at all. But before I go on to try to give some such positive account of colours I must bring into the open some considerations which make the Objectivist and Subjectivist views attractive, especially to those thinkers who do not bear in mind the scientific facts which make them unplausible.

The first consideration is that all the properties which science ascribes to physical objects seem to be purely relational.† Thus the length of the table on which I write would seem to consist in its relation to the metre bar in Paris, or perhaps to some chosen

* Different considerations which point to the same conclusion are given by the Earl of Halsbury in an article 'Epistemology and Communication Theory', *Philosophy*, Vol. 34, 1959, pp. 289–307.

† See the perceptive remarks by D. C. Williams, in an article, 'Mind as a Matter of Fact', *Review of Metaphysics*, Vol 13, 1959, pp. 203–25, especially p. 209. However, he takes up the opposite position to me. I prefer to put my money on scientific plausibility rather than on very abstruse metaphysical argument; even when I am not quite sure in what way the argument should be parried.

spectral wavelength. The notion of shape is not so obviously relational, but even so, it has to be defined in terms of length. For example, a square could be defined as a quadrangle whose sides are equal and whose diagonals are equal. A circle could be defined as a curve, every point of which is equidistant from a given point. When we pass from tables to sub-microscopic objects the position is no better. What properties has an electron, for example? The physicist would mention mass, charge, spin, etc. All these seem to consist in its relations to other things. So what is the electron in itself?

A further line of thought was suggested by Berkeley* and Hume.† Can you imagine something with the primary qualities alone? Could you, for example, imagine something with shape without filling in the shape with *colour*? (We must here, of course, include blacks, whites, greys, and the shimmering mixtures of blacks and whites that we see in a piece of transparent glass.) This quality, with which we fill in the shape, would appear to be an intrinsic, non-relational property either of the external object, which leads to the Objectivist view, or of the idea or sense datum, which leads to the Subjectivist view. If we take the latter alternative we are easily led, through the alleged inconceivability of anything with the primary qualities alone, to phenomenalism or to Berkeley's near-phenomenalism. This line of thought can be parried, but I pause to note an inconclusive reply to it by G. J. Warnock in his book on Berkeley.‡ Warnock points out that an invisible man is perfectly imaginable. Berkeley and Hume would surely agree that you can imagine an invisible man—for example, you might imagine a tray of drinks floating through the air as though carried by an invisible waiter. You can indeed imagine the invisible in that you can imagine queer things happening in the realm of the visible (and the audible, the tactual, etc.). This does not prove that you can imagine *everything* without colours or other secondary qualities. Hume has indeed given essentially this answer to Warnock in Book I, Part 4, Section 4, of the *Treatise on Human Nature*.

The correct reply to Berkeley and Hume is a different one. As Wittgenstein has cogently argued in his *Philosophical Investigations*

* Berkeley, *Principles of Human Knowledge*, § 10.
† Hume, *Treatise*, Bk. I, Part 4, Sec. 4.
‡ G. J. Warnock, *Berkeley* (Pelican Books, London, 1953), p. 101.

and other writings, we must not think of a word's having a meaning as its evoking a certain sort of mental image. Meaning has very little to do with imagery. If a man told you that he never had mental images you might think him of an unusual psychological type (but maybe there are such people). It would not lead you to say that his words were meaningless. Provided he utters his words intelligently and according to the correct rules (explicit or implicit) for their use, then he is speaking meaningfully. In some cases imagery may be even a hindrance to correct use (and hence meaningful utterance). It is, for example, impossible to imagine an electron. If we try to imagine one we perhaps call up the image of a rather fuzzy greyish sphere, and yet we know very well that it is absurd to ascribe colours or even shapes to electrons. Berkeley's objection fails because the meaning of a word consists in the way in which it is used, its *use*, not in its associated imagery.*

So far, so good. But have we answered the deeper objection which we noted earlier? Can a thing have relational properties only? There are three possibilities open to us here. In the first place we could explore the possibility of giving a theory of length, mass, and so on, as absolute and not relational. (To take account of the special theory of relativity we must understand by 'length' and 'mass' the rest length and rest mass.) My colleague C. B. Martin is wont to argue that we do indeed test propositions about length relationally, but that to go on to say that length is purely relational is to be unduly verificationist about meaning. In the second place we might challenge the principle that all the properties of a thing cannot be relational. In the third place we might say that an electron, for example, must have intrinsic qualities, and that all its known properties (such as length and mass) are nevertheless relational. Our knowledge of the physics and physiology of perception makes it implausible to say† that these intrinsic properties are to be identified with the *qualia* of sense perception. (I have argued that there are no such *qualia*.) There seems, however, to be no reason why we should not say that if an electron

* Cf. W. Kneale, *Probability and Induction* (Oxford University Press, 1949), p. 94. 'Berkeley pointed out quite correctly that the hypothetical entities of the physicists were unimaginable, but he concluded wrongly that because they were unimaginable they were inconceivable.' Also R. J. Hirst, *The Problems of Perception* (Allen and Unwin, London, 1959), p. 167, near bottom.

† As D. M. Armstrong has done, in his book *Perception and the Physical World* (Routledge and Kegan Paul, London, 1961), Chapter 15.

has to have non-relational properties, then these properties are properties of which we know nothing. ('Properties we know not what', to parody Locke.) In this way our metaphysical principle could be satisfied and no harm done.

We have seen that the idea that there must be intrinsic non-relational properties of things lends attractiveness to the theory of objective colour *qualia*. We have also seen that there are ways in which this attractiveness may be resisted. That it *should* be resisted is, of course, an implication of the considerations I have adduced earlier in this chapter. The theory of objective colour *qualia* is just fantastically implausible in the light of our scientific knowledge about colour vision. I shall now proceed to give a positive account of colours which eschews *qualia* altogether, whether external or internal. I do not claim any particular originality for it. It is a view which is, I think, at the back of the minds of many philosophers and psychologists but which I have not seen very explicitly stated. This is, perhaps, because it seems to them trite and obviously true. Unfortunately to other philosophers it appears obviously false, and so we must state it with some care, so as to avoid the objections of this second class of philosophers.

POSITIVE PHILOSOPHICAL THEORY OF COLOUR

It is sometimes said that a congenitally blind man cannot know the meaning of words such as 'red', 'green', and 'blue'. It will appear presently that there is very little truth in this, and that it would be far less misleading to say that a congenitally blind man could in fact know the meanings of these words just as well as his sighted brethren can.* To understand this is to understand the nub of the following account of colour concepts.

* P. T. Geach, in the excellent and instructive section on 'Abstractionism and Colour-Concepts' of his *Mental Acts* (Routledge and Kegan Paul, London, 1957), points out (pp. 33–8) that a man born blind can show a practical grasp of the logical grammar of colour words (p. 35), and also that he can grasp something of the aesthetic significance of colours in human life (p. 36). He points out important similarities between the blind man's and the sighted man's colour concepts, but I think that we can go even farther than Geach does in this direction. The question of a blind man's ability to use colour concepts is also raised in the dialogue between 'A' and 'B' on pp. 59–62 of J. Hospers' *Introduction to Philosophical Analysis* (Prentice-Hall, New York, 1953). The following pages should indicate how my view differs from B's, and how it avoids the objections put forward by A.

First of all it is necessary to introduce the notion of a *normal human percipient*. This must be done indirectly by means of a simpler notion, that of 'being more normal in a certain respect than . . .'. I shall say that a person *A* is more normal than a person *B* with respect to a certain type of colour discrimination if he can discriminate things of a certain sort with respect to colour while *B* cannot do so.

This move will at once strike some people as circular. For I am proposing to analyse colour concepts by means of the notion 'discriminate with respect to colour'. However, there is not really a circularity here, any more than there is in Whitehead's and Russell's definition (in *Principia Mathematica*) of number *via* the notion 'equinumerous'. Just as the notion 'equinumerous' can be elucidated with a smaller logical apparatus than is needed for the concept of 'number', so (as we shall see) the notion of 'discriminate with respect to colour' can be analysed with less conceptual apparatus than is needed for the full concept of colour.

Suppose that you have a lot of pieces of wool and that each of these pieces of wool is tagged in some secret way known only to yourself. You then try an experiment with two people *P* and *Q*. You get these people in turn to sort the wool into various bundles, and then after mixing up the wool again you repeat the experiment. By looking at the tags, which are, as I said, unknown to *P* and *Q*, you find that *P* and *Q* always sort the wool into the same bundles. You also find that this ability to sort into bundles is adversely affected when instead of illuminating the wool with daylight you illuminate the wool with monochromatic light, for example sodium light. So it is clear that the wool is not being sorted in respect of texture, for example. Nor is it being sorted out by touch, taste, or non-visual sense. Nor is it because the pieces of wool reflect different amounts of light. The difference is not that between *bright* and *dark*. (In fact, you can antecedently make sure that the wool is alike in texture, etc., different only in colour, but this need not enter into the analysis. Tests such as illuminating in sodium light will in principle serve our purpose, without bringing in the notion of 'differing only in colour'.) You find that *P* can sort the wool into more bundles than *Q* can. We then say that *P* can discriminate with respect to colour things which *Q* cannot so discriminate.

It would be tedious to go into more detail, but it should be clear from the foregoing paragraph that with ingenuity we can elucidate the complex expression 'discriminate with respect to colour', as it occurs in any context, without making use of colour words or of the general word 'colour' itself. It should be noticed, moreover, that there is no need to use colour words in our instructions to the wool sorters. We might simply say to them 'Sort out the wool into bundles that appear to you to differ from one another in some obvious way'. We have so arranged the experiment that the only obvious differences between the pieces of wool are colour differences, but we need not say so. Or if we did, we could say so without using colour language: we might, for example, describe the differences as those which no longer remain obvious in sodium light, or in twilight.

We now define 'a normal percipient'. A normal percipient is one who is at least as normal in respect of any colour discrimination as is any other percipient. Thus, if A can make discriminations with respect to colour that B cannot make, then B is not a normal percipient. It may well be, of course, that there are not in fact any normal percipients. For A may make better discriminations than anyone else at the red end of the spectrum, and B may make better discriminations than anyone else at the blue end of the spectrum. In this case a normal percipient would be an imaginary person who combined the abilities of both A and B. (Or, if you prefer, the notion could be realised by a syndicate consisting of A and B acting in concert.) However, this is an unimportant subtlety. Within a small margin of error, there are in fact many millions of normal percipients.

If we have a child who is a normal percipient, or nearly a normal percipient, we can set about teaching him how to use words such as 'red', 'blue', and 'green' by a direct ostensive process. We can teach him to respond with 'red' when he is confronted with ripe tomatoes, geraniums, and British post boxes, with the word 'blue' when he is confronted with forget-me-nots and delphiniums. Of course, these particular objects need not be chosen. Different pupils learn colour words by being confronted with different sorts of things. The important point is that in learning colour words, if we are approximately normal percipients, we are taught (or encouraged) to make various discriminations and to couple the verbal reactions of saying 'red', 'green', 'blue', etc., in a determinate way with these discriminatory reactions. (I have said

77

'taught or encouraged' in the last sentence because it seems to me that some abilities to discriminate colour are anterior to teaching and language, while other discriminations have to be taught.) Thus, 'green' will be applied to all things of a set which are hard to distinguish from one another with respect to colour, whereas the things we call 'blue' and 'yellow' are in general easier to distinguish with respect to colour from members of this set: that is, they can be distinguished from the green things in relatively unfavourable conditions in which the green things cannot be distinguished from one another. Of course, there will be some things which are as hard to distinguish from some green things as they are to distinguish from some yellow things: these we may call 'greenish yellow'.

What about the differences between Oxford blue and Cambridge blue? (Dark blue and light blue.) We call things of both these colours 'blue', but they are nevertheless from the present point of view different colours. A normal percipient will easily distinguish otherwise similar objects, one of which is Oxford blue and the other of which is Cambridge blue. When we become more scientific we can refine our language and say that Oxford and Cambridge blue are of the same *hue* but different *saturations*. (You can turn an Oxford-blue light source into a Cambridge-blue one by mixing in white light.)

Now consider two similar objects, such as rowing oars, one of which is one colour (Oxford blue or green, perhaps) and the other is another colour (Cambridge blue or red, perhaps). You may object to my analysis of colours in terms of discriminatory reactions by saying that a man who distinguishes the one object from the other does so *because he sees that they are of different colours*. Have I not therefore put the cart before the horse? This objection is easily rebutted. It is important to recall that I took pains to elucidate the expression 'discriminate with respect to colour' without making use of the notion of 'colour'. It is perfectly true that the man who distinguishes the two things does so *because he sees that they are of different colours*. To say this is to deny that he distinguishes the two things because of shape or texture or smell, for example, and to assert that his discrimination is a 'discrimination with respect to colour' in the already elucidated sense, the sense which does *not* presuppose the notion of colour.

I do not wish to deny, of course, that a man who sees an Oxford-blue oar has a different sort of visual experience from that had by a man who sees a Cambridge-blue oar. In the next chapter I shall defend the view that experiences are in fact brain processes. The importance of this lies in the fact that, if I am right, I can admit experiences without, like the Subjectivist, putting them unplausibly outside a unified scientific world outlook. However, for the purpose of the present chapter our visual experiences are of secondary importance: with a qualification to be mentioned shortly we may say that provided that a man's discriminatory reactions are correct, then, so far as his grasp of colours is concerned, his experiences can be what they please.

We might say, as a first shot, that 'this is red' means roughly that a normal human percipient would not easily pick this thing out of a heap of geranium petals, though he would easily pick it out of a heap of lettuce leaves.* That this is not quite right follows from the fact that a person can certainly know the meaning of the word 'red' without knowing the words 'geranium' or 'lettuce', not to mention 'normal percipient'. Nevertheless, we could imagine that definitions of this sort are given to a tribe of people who had grown up knowing English but without having ever been introduced to colour vocabulary. These definitions would in fact lead these people to use colour words very much as we, who learned them ostensively, do use them. It is not even very unnatural to regard such a phrase as 'the colour of tomatoes' as a definition of 'red'. (Something very similar is to be found in the *Concise Oxford English Dictionary*.) What we get is admittedly not an explicit definition or translation of 'red'. Nevertheless, it is a perfectly good instruction for someone who knows the word 'colour', but who for some queer reason, or perhaps because he is a foreigner learning English, does not know the word 'red'. It is but one step further to imagine people who introduce the notion of colour itself by means of the notion of the abilities to discriminate of normal percipients.

Imagine a race of congenitally blind people who have as slaves a race of normal percipients. There is a system of taboo whereby the slaves must never use colour words, so that they themselves never utter them or learn to understand them when they are uttered by others. The blind people cut up wool into hundreds of

* As I suggest in my paper 'Sensations and Brain Processes', *Philosophical Review*, Vol. 68, 1959, pp. 141–56.

pieces and dip different bits of wool into different dyes. (One dye to each bit of wool, but many bits of wool to each dye.) They then do experiments on the slaves and discover their discrimination patterns with respect to the bits of wool. We can suppose that the bits of wool are tagged in some way which is unknown to the slaves, and that the slaves assort the bits of wool into various heaps. The pieces are then shuffled up together again, and it is found that when the slaves sort out the wool again they always put the bits of wool into the same heaps that they did before. The slaves can distinguish bits of wool from different heaps but not bits of wool from the same heap. More refined experiments with more dyes, better light, and more time would, of course, lead not to a small set of heaps, but to a very large number of heaps, leading to the idea of a colour continuum: the blind man would say that the colour of bit of wool B is between the colours of bits of wool A and C if a slave can distinguish A from C but not A from B or B from C.

The blind rulers could invent words 'α', 'β', 'γ', etc., for the various classes of pieces of wool which the slaves cannot easily distinguish from one another. They then find that a piece of α wool is not easily picked out by a slave when it is dropped into a bowl of tomatoes, and β wool is not easily picked out by a slave when it is dropped into a bowl of lemons. They assign the word 'red' to α wool, 'yellow' to β wool, and so on. Further details can be left to the reader. Such a tribe of congenitally blind people could come to use the words 'red', 'yellow', and so on very much as we do. But they would not have learned the words ostensively. (Remember that the slaves have no colour vocabulary.)

Should we say that the blind rulers mean the same by colour words as we do? It is surely more misleading to say that they do not than that they do. It is true that the blind rulers do not react spontaneously with 'red' when they are confronted by a tomato, for of course they cannot see the tomato. Nevertheless, the objective criteria for the redness of an object are exactly the same with them as with us. These objective criteria are the discriminatory responses of normal percipients. As against the common view that colour words must be meaningless to the congenitally blind, I would rather say, therefore, that the congenitally blind could in fact understand the meanings of colour words every bit as well as sighted people can. A congenitally blind man cannot, and never could, use himself as one of the normal percipients (or 'colour meters', one might say), but has to use someone else. This is only to say that the blind man is not a normal percipient, which is trivial. The idea that a congenitally blind man could not understand colour words is connected, I think, with a pre-Wittgensteinian view of meaning not as 'use' but as some sort of mental experience, which evokes and is evoked by a word.

Having so far given an account of colours which depends on behavioural reactions and which plays down our inner experiences as unimportant, I must now slightly qualify this. The account I have given is, I believe, very nearly true, but something more needs to be said. The following case, which was suggested to me by C. B. Martin, brings this out clearly. Martin supposes that the colours of everything in the universe suddenly were to change in a systematic manner. It will be recollected (see p. 67 above) that we can map any colour which is in position P on the colour circle into the colour Q which is at the same distance diametrically opposite to it from the position of white. White is mapped into itself, and all other colours are correlated in this way with one and only one other colour. Suppose that a sudden change occurs in the universe, so that the colours of things change into the colours with which they are correlated in the above mapping. Let us suppose that tomatoes become blue, delphiniums red, grass violet, and so on. We suppose also that the light that comes to be reflected from tomatoes is like that which is now reflected from delphiniums, and vice-versa. (*I.e.* the above sudden change could be detected by scientific measurements.) Our inner experiences will change too: those caused by tomatoes will be like those which were previously caused in us by delphiniums, and vice-versa. With this sudden systematic change in the colours of things the pattern of discriminatory reactions of normal percipients will remain the same as before. Tomatoes will still be easily picked out from delphiniums, but not easily from strawberries. Nevertheless, it does seem to make sense to say that the colours of things had changed, and indeed we can imagine to ourselves what a systematic change of this sort would be like.

On the level of science there would be a simple criterion for saying that the colours of things had changed. This would be that spectrometers would show that the sort of light reflected from tomatoes was now approximately the sort that used to be reflected from delphiniums, and vice-versa (etc., etc.). (The supposition of a sudden universal change like this would, of course, lead to incoherencies in science, but we can let this pass, since we are dealing with a purely fanciful possibility.) But on the level of common sense, too, and quite apart from measurements of light waves, we could say that the colours of things had changed in a systematic way. This would be because, for example, the inner experiences that we now got from tomatoes would be like those that we previously got from delphiniums, and vice-versa. We would tend to classify our memories of tomato experiences with our present perceptual experiences of delphiniums, and vice-versa. Moreover, our brains would cause the word 'red' to come to our lips when we now looked at delphiniums, and 'blue' when we looked at tomatoes. We should be matching our present experiences of seeing tomatoes with our remembered experiences of seeing delphiniums, and vice-versa. In the next chapter I shall argue that experiences are brain processes, and that they have no *qualia*, and so there is not a difficulty for me here. What would happen in the case supposed by Martin is that if P is the sort of light reflected from tomatoes and Q is the sort of light reflected from delphiniums, and if M is the sort of inner experience (brain process) caused by P and N is the one caused by Q, then suddenly tomatoes cause Q and N and delphiniums cause P and M. Because of our ability to match our inner experiences by means of memory, we could detect this change, even though the various changes of colours were such as to cause no change in our patterns of behavioural discriminations. It is therefore not *quite* true that our inner experiences do not matter at all for the analysis of our colour concepts. It still remains true, however, that it does not matter at all whether the inner experience produced in *you* by a tomato or a lemon is at all like that produced in *me* by a tomato or a lemon. *By and large*, our concepts can be analysed behaviouristically, but *not quite*. (Nevertheless, the purely behaviouristic account is almost the truth, much nearer the truth than the Objectivist and Subjectivist view considered earlier in this chapter.) Our inner experiences are certainly of *very little* importance for our colour concepts. A man without any inner experiences of colour at all, but who made all the right discriminatory responses, would in fact get on pretty well in talking about colours with us. Martin's case is important in showing that one must nevertheless not be too behaviouristic. I must ask the reader to concede for the moment that I can talk about inner experiences (as brain processes) and that I do not need to ascribe to them any *qualia* or properties which cannot be dealt with in a physicalist way. The justification of this will, as I have said, come in the next chapter.

Another instructive objection to my analysis of colours has been put forward to me by M. C. Bradley. Suppose, says Bradley, that a man makes all the discriminatory responses that I do but that everything looks grey to him. Is this not conceivable? I would agree with Bradley that this is a logically possible case, but one must exercise a great deal of caution in the manner in which one describes it in detail. If our tendencies to discriminate and not to discriminate were causally bound up with inner experiences (brain processes), could they then be the undifferentiated experience of seeing grey? The experience of seeing uniform grey is not an experience of making sharp discriminations. Bradley's case would have therefore to be described as follows: one unconsciously makes colour discriminations while all the time having a conscious experience (brain process) just like that which we have when seeing grey. Of course if Bradley's case were the rule we would be unable to describe the experience as one of seeing grey, for there would be no objective criterion for *being* grey. Bradley's case is, however, valuable in that it, like Martin's, shows that our ordinary concept of colour is rather rich, though its essential core is analysable in terms of discriminatory responses. It reminds us that there are such things as visual experiences (experiences of colour). Nevertheless, in the world as it in fact is, men who had no inner colour experiences but who made all the appropriate behavioural discriminations could talk about colours as intelligibly as we could. The behaviouristic analysis of colours is almost right, and the next chapter will provide the tools for making it completely right, and yet without departing from the physicalist outlook of this chapter.

We saw earlier that the human visual mechanism behaves rather like an arrangement of three photo-electric cells, though with additional complications. Let us call such an arrangement of photo-electric cells '*P*'. Let us consider another arrangement of cells, which we will call '*Q*', with the following property. *P* distinguishes different mixtures of light waves from one another that Q does not distinguish, and Q distinguishes mixtures that P does not distinguish. It may be that there are beings (perhaps extra-terrestrial ones) which are like Q. This bears out my contention that colour concepts correspond to the distinctions made by a rather complex neurophysiological mechanism and do not corres-pond to anything simple in nature. This accounts for the fact, often remarked on by philosophers, of the scientific unimportance and causal inefficacy of colours. We should not expect to find simple laws relating to colours, except when the mixtures of colours are fairly simply related to spectral wavelength. (Thus, it is indeed useful to talk of 'red' and 'blue' stars, for in this case the stars send out mostly long-waved and mostly short-waved light respec-tively. We must remember that this sort of situation does not necessarily obtain. We can get a perfectly good colour by, say, mixing arbitrary proportions of five arbitrarily chosen wave-lengths, or in even more idiosyncratic ways.) Boyle, in his *Origin of Forms and Qualities* (1666),* most instructively compares the secondary qualities to the power of a key to turn a lock. This clearly depends as much on the lock as on the key, and we cannot expect such a power to depend in any simple way on the shape of the key. Moreover, we can imagine a complicated lock such that keys of various different and queer shapes fit it and there is here quite obviously no one–one correlation between the similarity in shapes of the keys and similarity of their lock-turning powers.

We can see, then, that colour is an anthropocentric concept. Extraterrestrial beings could be expected to have a similar concept of length or electric charge to ours, but we would not expect their colour concepts, supposing that they had any, to correspond to ours in any simple manner. If our philosophical task is, in part, to see the world *sub specie aeternitatis*, to see the world in such a way as to discount our idiosyncratic, human, terrestrial perspec-tive, then we must eschew the concepts of colour and other secondary qualities.

OTHER SECONDARY QUALITIES

What about the other secondary qualities, such as those of sound, smell, taste, and of hot and cold? Some of these are not quite so

---

* If it is not easy to consult this work there are useful quotations from it to be found in the article by Reginald Jackson, already mentioned.

anthropocentric as colour. Consider our sense of hot and cold (or more properly, of temperature).* This is less anthropocentric than our colour sense because the human being is much more like an (inefficient) thermometer than he is like an (inefficient) spectrometer. If a man puts his finger into two different pails of water he can, fairly reliably, tell which has the higher temperature. Of course his reliability in this respect falls far short of that of a thermometer. Philosophy students have long been aware of the fact that a man who has put his hand in hot water will feel tepid water as cool, whereas if his hand has just been in cold water he will judge the tepid water to be warm. He will be inclined both ways at once if he performs this operation simultaneously with his left and right hands. Similarly, a man will tend to judge a piece of iron (which conducts heat away from his skin) to be colder than a piece of wood, even though the temperatures of the iron and the wood are in fact identical. In short, we are unreliable thermometers, and we are easily put out of order and made even more unreliable. But our judgments of hot and cold are closely related to the judgments we make by means of a thermometer: we know how to test for our unreliabilities, and so long as we do not need too much accuracy we can use ourselves (or other people) as rather inaccurate thermometers. In this way our temperature sense differs from our visual sense: we are nowhere near to being even inaccurate spectrometers.

Our sense of sound is less closely related to physical properties than our temperature sense, but is more closely related than is our visual sense. As far as single notes are concerned some people have almost as good a sense of relative pitch as we could have using a physical instrument. However, they hear chords as wholes, and only through a course of musical training can they learn to say what the individual notes of a chord are. Furthermore, sounds which consist of in effect an infinite number of simple wavelengths (say the noise of a nail being scratched on wood, or any spoken phoneme) are heard as wholes and the reactions of percipients are not relatable in any simple way to occurrences in nature.

Some of the things we have said about colour could certainly carry over here. Nevertheless, our sound sense is tied a little more

* On the perception of heat, see the article by Colin Strang: 'The Perception of Heat', *Proceedings of the Aristotelian Society*, Vol. 61, 1960–61, pp. 239–52.

closely to what goes on in nature in this way: sounds do not 'mix' to the extent that colours do. If I shine two colours on to a screen you see a third colour. However, if I make a noise by scratching a nail on wood and another simultaneous noise by rubbing my finger on glass you can still hear the two sounds as distinguishable noises.*

The secondary qualities of taste and smell are in some ways not so anthropocentric as that of colour. They are, of course, powers to cause discriminatory reactions, and these discriminations do relate to fairly specific differences in the chemistry of the things tasted or smelt. However, in the *range* of such discriminations tastes and smells *are* anthropocentric. The range of sorts of chemicals which cause taste and smell reactions in human beings is pretty certainly specific to the human species.

But when all is said and done, all secondary quality concepts concern the classifications of sensory stimuli made by complex neurophysiological mechanisms. There is no reason to expect a close correspondence between these classifications and the way things in fact are in nature. Indeed, in the case of colour we saw how slight this correspondence is. One of the few modern writers on the philosophy of perception to have remarked on this is F. A. Hayek. In his book *The Sensory Order*† he has an illuminating example of a machine which places balls with diameters of 16, 18, 28, 31, and 32 millimetres respectively in a receptacle marked 'A' and balls with a diameter of 17, 22, 30, and 35 in a receptacle marked 'B'. In this case the fact that the machine places a ball into a particular receptacle is the only criterion for assigning it to a certain class.

Some of our classifications, especially of tastes and smells, may be very crude. Thus, most of us are more willing to say that a smell is 'nice' or 'nasty' than that it is the smell of roses or jasmine. The words 'nice' and 'nasty' clearly lead us from the realm of discriminatory reactions to those of inner experiences. I have not denied the existence of inner experiences, such as the experience of having a sense datum of a certain sort. They simply have not

---

* For further light on this, and a discussion of contrary-to-fact physical conditions and unusual nervous systems whereby colours would be seen together much as sounds can be heard together, see my article 'Incompatible Colors', *Philosophical Studies*, Vol. 10, 1959, pp. 39–42.

† Routledge and Kegan Paul, London, 1952. See p. 49.

been necessary in most of my analysis. This leads on to the next chapter, in which I attempt to give an account of inner experiences as brain processes. In particular, I try to show how I can avoid attributing any non-physical properties (such as unanalysable *qualia*) to these inner experiences.

V

CONSCIOUSNESS

IN the last chapter I have talked often enough about the *discriminatory responses* which human beings *make*. I have postponed discussion of the *experiences* they *have*. Discussion of the nature of experiences was not important for our examination of the secondary qualities, which I elucidated as powers to cause differential responses. I did not want to deny that we have experiences. I do want to argue, however, that these can be elucidated within the physicalist framework. In this chapter I wish to argue for the view that conscious experiences are simply *brain processes*. This is a view which almost every elementary student of philosophy is taught to refute. I shall try to show that the standard refutations of the view are fallacious.

Many of our ordinary psychological concepts seem to refer to inner processes. Of course this is not so with all of them. Some of them seem to be able to be elucidated in a behaviouristic way: to say that someone is vain is to say that he tends to show off, or look at himself often in the mirror, or something of that sort. To say that he is interested in mathematics is to say that he has a tendency to read mathematical books, to work out problems, to talk in terms of mathematical analogies, and so on. Similarly with the emotions: 'anger', 'fear', 'joy', and the like can plausibly be said to refer to characteristic behaviour patterns. Again various adverbial phrases can be elucidated in a behaviouristic way. As Ryle* has pointed out, the phrase 'thinking what he is doing' in

* *Concept of Mind* (Hutchinson, London, 1949), pp. 135–49.

'he is driving the car thinking what he is doing' refers to certain tendencies to behave in various ways: for example, to apply the brakes when one sees a child about to run on to the road. To drive a car thinking what you are doing is not like walking and whistling. You can walk without whistling and you can whistle without walking, but you cannot do the 'thinking what you are doing' part of 'driving the car thinking what you are doing' without the driving of the car. (Similarly, you can walk gracefully, but you cannot do the being graceful part of the performance without doing the walking part of it.) This helps to elucidate the well-known difficulty of thinking without words. Certain kinds of thinking are pieces of intelligent talking to oneself. Consider the way in which I 'thinkingly' wrote the last sentence. I can no more do the 'thinking' part without the talking (or writing) part than a man can do the being graceful part apart from the walking (or some equivalent activity).

If all our psychological concepts were capable of a behaviouristic or quasi-behaviouristic analysis this would be congenial for physicalism. (I say 'or quasi-behaviouristic' here because I would prefer to say, for example, that fear is the state of a person which is the causal condition of the characteristic behaviour pattern, rather than as with Ryle that it is the behaviour pattern. In the light of modern knowledge we can also say that the state in question is a neural state, but this fact need not enter into the analysis. Socrates did not know this fact, though he had the concept of fear.) Unfortunately, however, there are a good many psychological concepts for which a behaviouristic account seems impossible.

Suppose that I report that I am having an orange-yellow roundish after-image. Or suppose again that I report that I have a pain. It seems clear that the content of my report cannot be exclusively a set of purely behavioural facts. There seems to be some element of 'pure inner experience' which is being reported, and to which only I have direct access. You can observe my behaviour, but only I can be aware of my own after-image or my own pain. I suspect that the notion of a 'pain' is partly akin to that of an emotion: that is, the notion of pain seems essentially to involve the notion of distress, and distress is perhaps capable of an elucidation in terms of a characteristic behaviour pattern. But this is not all that a pain is: there is an immediately felt sensation which we do not have in other cases of distress. (Consider by contrast the distress of a mother because her son goes out gambling. The son gives his mother much pain, but he does not necessarily give her *a* pain.) In the case of the after-image there is not this 'emotional' component of distress, and it seems easier to consider such 'neat' inner experiences. I shall therefore concentrate on the case where I report the experience of having an after-image.

Suppose, then, that I report that I am having a yellowish-orange after-image. What is it that I am reporting? It looks at first sight uncomfortably as if I am reporting a private occurrence, different in kind from those which the physicist or the neurophysiologist can observe. I say 'uncomfortably as if', because if these private occurrences were non-physical in nature they would be 'nomological danglers', and the laws whereby they would dangle would be unplausible for the very same reasons which were mentioned in the last chapter in connection with subjective colour *qualia*. We would appear to have *ultimate* laws of nature which relate something simple, or apparently simple, such as an experience, to a very complex and special neuro-physiological process involving billions of neurons. As I remarked earlier, we expect ultimate laws of nature to relate simple, or at any rate homogeneous, entities.

One way out of the difficulty might be to argue that a putative report such as 'I am having a yellowish-orange after-image' is not really a report, and that consequently there is no problem about what is reported by such an utterance. This view, which is perhaps Wittgenstein's and is almost certainly Ryle's in the *Concept of Mind*, may be developed as follows. When I say that it looks to me that there is a roundish yellowish-orange patch on the wall I am expressing some sort of temptation to say that there *is* a roundish yellowish-orange patch on the wall. Similarly, when I 'report' a pain I am really not reporting anything at all but am doing a sort of wince. As Wittgenstein says, 'The verbal expression of pain replaces crying and does not describe it.'* (Nor, as I interpret Wittgenstein, does it describe anything else.) As I have said earlier, I prefer to consider the case of the after-image, since part of what we 'report' when we 'report' pain may be distress, and it

* L. Wittgenstein, *Philosophical Investigations* (Blackwell, Oxford, 1953). See §§ 244, 367, 370.

is possible to elucidate distress in a behaviourist or near behaviourist way. Even so, there is an ingredient in pain, the 'neat' experience, which *prima-facie* is not so explicable. It is tempting, then, to say that the report of the neat experience, anyway, is not really a report, though it looks grammatically like one. It is on this view more like 'ouch', a remark which it would be absurd to call 'true' or 'false'. (It can be sincere, or insincere, genuine or feigned.) The 'report' of the yellowish-orange after-image, it is tempting to say, is similarly the expression of a temptation to say that there *is* a yellowish-orange something on the wall. Note that the expression of a temptation is not a report that I have the temptation. Compare the case where I say 'Come on, varsity'; I am expressing a desire that the University team should win, though I am not making an autobiographical assertion that I have this desire. In Ryle's terminology, what I do is not to make an assertion but to make an avowal.*

If all first-person psychological 'reports' could be shown to be merely avowals there would be no problem about the mysterious nature of the putative objects of these 'reports'. The 'expressive' or 'avowal' theory is therefore very congenial to me. However, it is hard to accept it. It does seem simply obvious, a matter of fact, that we do report something, in a perfectly full-blooded sense of 'report', when we tell the dentist that we have a pain or the psychologist that we are having an after-image. I propose therefore to give an account of reports of immediate experience which accepts that they are genuine reports. It will avoid the unpalatable consequences of psychophysical dualism because it will assert that the goings on which are reported are in fact brain processes. This view has, of course, been opposed by apparently decisive philosophical objections. Almost every first-year student of philosophy would claim to be able to refute it. Nevertheless, it will, I hope, turn out that these objections can be rebutted. They are by no means as cogent as is commonly thought. I first came to realise the possibilities of the brain process view from my one-time colleague U. T. Place, who published an excellent article on the subject in the *British Journal of Psychology*.† H. Feigl has also argued at greater length and in the same direction,‡ and I myself have

* See his discussion of 'avowals', *op. cit.,* p. 102.

† 'Is Consciousness a Brain Process?' *British Journal of Psychology,* Vol. 47, 1956, pp. 44–50.

‡ *Op. cit.*

elsewhere recapitulated some of Place's and Feigl's arguments and added some of my own.*

THE BRAIN PROCESS THEORY

The first argument against the identification of experiences and brain processes can be put as follows: Aristotle, or for that matter an illiterate peasant, can report his images and aches and pains, and yet nevertheless may not know that the brain has anything to do with thinking. (Aristotle thought that the brain was an organ for cooling the blood.) Therefore what Aristotle or the peasant reports cannot *be* a brain process, though it can, of course, be something which is (unknown to Aristotle or the peasant) causally connected with a brain process.

The reply to this argument is simply this: when I say that experiences are brain processes I am asserting this *as a matter of fact*. I am not asserting that 'brain process' is part of what we *mean* by 'experience'. A couple of analogies will show what is wrong with the argument. Suppose that a man is acquainted with Sir Walter Scott and knows him as 'the author of *Waverley*'. He may never have heard of Ivanhoe. Yet the author of *Waverley* can be (and was) the very same person as the author of *Ivanhoe*. Again, consider lightning.† According to modern science, lightning is a movement of electric charges from one ionised layer of cloud to another such layer or to the earth. This is what lightning really is. This fact was not known to Aristotle. And yet Aristotle presumably knew the meaning of the Greek work for 'lightning' perfectly well.

I wish to make it clear that I have used these examples mainly to make a *negative* point: I do not wish to claim that the relation

* 'Sensations and Brain Processes', *Philosophical Review*, Vol. 68, 1959, pp. 141–56. See also discussion by Stevenson, *ibid.*, Vol. 69, 1960, pp. 505–10, and my reply, *ibid.*, Vol. 70, 1961, pp. 406–7. Also discussion notes by G. Pitcher and W. D. Joske in *Australasian Journal of Philosophy*, Vol. 38, 1960, pp. 150–7, and my reply, *ibid.*, pp. 252–4, and by Kurt Baier, *ibid.*, Vol. 40, 1962, pp. 57–68, and my reply, *ibid.*, pp. 68–70. See also Hilary Putnam, 'Minds and Machines', in Sidney Hook (ed.), *Dimensions of Mind* (Collier, New York, 1961). A physicalist theory of sense impressions was defended by H. Reichenbach in his *Experience and Prediction* (University of Chicago Press, 1938).

† Place, *op. cit.*, p. 47; Feigl, *op. cit.*, p. 438.

between the expression 'I am having an after image' and 'there is such-and-such a brain process going on in me' is in *all* respects like that between 'there is the author of *Waverley*' and 'there is the author of *Ivanhoe*', or like that between 'that is lightning' and 'that is a motion of electric charges'. The point I wish to make at present is simply that these analogies show the weakness of the above argument against identifying experiences and brain processes. I am, however, suggesting also that it may be the true nature of our inner experiences, as revealed by science, to be brain processes, just as to be a motion of electric charges is the true nature of lightning, what lightning really is. Neither the case of lightning nor the case of inner experiences is like that of explaining a footprint by reference to a burglar. It is not the true nature of a footprint to be a burglar.

In short, there can be contingent statements of the form 'A is identical with B', and a person may know that something is an A without knowing it is a B. An illiterate peasant might well be able to talk about his sensations without knowing about his brain processes, just as he can talk about lightning, though he knows nothing about electricity. I should, moreover, like to make it clear that by 'lightning' I mean the publicly observable physical object lightning, not a visual sense datum. The sense datum, or rather the having of the sense datum, may well on my view be a correlate of the electric discharge. For on my view the having of the sense datum is the brain process that is *caused* by the lightning. But the physical object lightning *is* the electric discharge, and is not just a correlate of it.

A related objection which is sometimes put up against the brain process thesis runs as follows. It will be pointed out that the hypothesis that sensations are connected with brain processes shares the tentative character of all scientific hypotheses. It is possible, though in the highest degree unlikely, that our present physiological theories will one day be given up, and it will seem as absurd to connect sensations with the brain as it now does to connect them with the heart. It follows that when we report a sensation we are not reporting a brain process.

This argument falls to the ground once it is realised that assertions of identity can be factual and contingent. The argument certainly does prove that when I say 'I have a yellowish-orange after-image' I cannot *mean* that I have such-and-such a brain process. (Any more than that if a man says 'there goes the author of *Waverley*' he *means* 'there goes the author of *Ivanhoe*'. The two sentences are not inter-translatable.) But the argument does not prove that what we report (*e.g.* the having of an after-image) is not *in fact* a brain process. It could equally be said that it is conceivable (though in the highest degree unlikely) that the electrical theory of lightning should be given up. This shows indeed that 'that is lightning' does not *mean* the same as 'that is a motion of electric charges'. But for all that, lightning is *in fact* a motion of electric charges.

It may be objected that even if I can get out of saying that sensations or experiences are entities over and above brain processes I can do so only at the cost of admitting 'emergent' or irreducibly non-physical *properties* of brain processes. If this objection can be substantiated it is a very serious one, for, as we saw in Chapter IV, emergent properties would be just as much objectionable nomological danglers as psychical *entities* are. I think I can rebut the objection, and I wish to make it quite clear that I wish to rebut it. The present theory is *not* the well-known 'double-aspect' theory. According to this theory, we are immediately aware, in inner experience, of certain 'aspects' or 'qualities' of the neural processes, and the inner aspects are in principle quite distinct from those aspects which are open to the neurophysiologist or other external observer. Now it may be said* that if we identify an experience and a brain process and if this identification is, as I hold it is, a *contingent* or *factual* one, then the experience must be identified as having some property not logically deducible from the properties whereby we identify the brain process. To return to our analogy of the contingent identification of the author of *Waverley* with the author of *Ivanhoe*. If the property of being the author of *Waverley* is the analogue of the neurophysiological properties of a brain process, what is the analogue of the property of being author of *Ivanhoe*? There is an inclination to say: 'an irreducible, emergent, introspectible property'.

How do I get round this objection? I do so as follows. The man who reports a yellowish-orange after-image does so in effect as follows: '*What is going on in me is like what is going on in me when* my eyes are open, the lighting is normal, etc., etc., and there really is a yellowish-orange patch on the wall.' In this sentence

* As by Professor Max Black, in discussion.

the word 'like' is meant to be used in such a way that something can be like itself: an identical twin is not only like his brother but is like himself too. With this sense of 'like' the above formula will do for a report that one is having a veridical sense datum too. Notice that the italicised words *what is going on in me is like what is going on in me when . . .* are topic-neutral. A dualist will think that what is going on in him when he reports an experience is in fact a non-physical process (though his report does not say that it is), an ancient Greek may think that it is a process in his heart, and I think that it is a process in my brain. The report itself is neutral to all these possibilities. This extreme 'openness' and 'topic neutrality' of reports of experiences perhaps explains why the 'raw feels' or immediate qualia of internal experiences have seemed so elusive. 'What is going on in me is like what is going on in me when . . .' is a colourless phrase, just as the word 'somebody' is colourless. If I say 'somebody is coming through the garden' I may do so because I see my wife coming through the garden. Because of the colourless feel of the word 'somebody' a very naïve hearer (like the king in *Alice in Wonderland*, who got thoroughly confused over the logical grammar of 'nobody') might suspect that 'somebody is coming through the garden' is about some very elusive and ghostly entity, instead of, in fact, that very colourful and flesh and blood person, my wife.

For this account to be successful, it is necessary that we should be able to report two processes as like one another without being able to say in what respect they are alike. An experience of having an after-image may be classified as like the experience I have when I see an orange, and this likeness, on my view, must consist in a similarity of neuro-physiological pattern. But of course we are not immediately aware of the pattern; at most we are able to report the similarity. Now it is tempting, when we think in a metaphysical and *a priori* way, to suppose that reports of similarities can be made only on a basis of the conscious apprehension of the features in respect of which these similarities subsist. But when we think objectively about the human being as a functioning mechanism this metaphysical supposition may come to seem unwarranted. It is surely more easy to construct a mechanism which will record (on a punched tape, for example) bare similarities in a class of stimuli than it is to construct a machine which will provide a report of the features in which these similarities consist. It therefore seems to me quite possible that we should be able to make reports to the effect that 'what is going on in me is like what goes on in me when . . .' without having any idea whatever of what in particular is going on in me (*e.g.* whether a brain process, a heart process, or a spiritual process).

I must make it clear that I am not producing the phrase 'What is going on in me is like what goes on in me when . . .' as a *translation* of a sensation report. It is rather meant to give in an informal way what a sensation report purports to be about. For example, it has been objected that it is no good translating 'I have a pain' as 'what is going on in me is like what goes on when a pin is stuck into me', since, to put it crudely, pains have nothing in particular to do with pins, and certainly someone might learn the word 'pain' without ever having learned the word 'pin'. When, however, I say that 'I have a pain' is to the effect of 'what is going on in me is like what goes on in me when a pin is stuck into me', my intention is simply to indicate the way in which learning to make sensation reports is learning to report likenesses and un-likenesses of various internal processes. There is indeed no need to learn the word 'pain' by having a pin stuck into one. A child may, for example, be introduced to the word 'pain' when he accidentally grazes his knee. But sensation talk must be learned with reference to some environmental stimulus situation or another. Certainly it need not be any *particular* one, such as the sticking in of pins.

The above considerations also show how we can reply to another objection which is commonly brought against the brain-process theory. The experience, it will be said, is not in physical space, whereas the brain process is. Hence the experience is not a brain process. This objection seems to beg the question. If my view is correct the experience *is* in physical space: in my brain. The truth behind the objection is that the experience is not re-ported as something spatial. It is reported only (in effect) in terms of 'what is going on in me is like what goes on in me when . . .'. This report is so 'open' and general that it is indeed neutral between my view that what goes on in me goes on in physical space and the psychophysical dualist's view that what goes on in me goes on in a non-spatial entity. This is without prejudice to the statement that what goes on in me is something which in fact *is* in physical space. On my view sensations do in fact have all sorts of neurophysiological properties. For they are neurophysiological processes. But the specifically neurophysiological properties are not mentioned in the sensation report, which is 'open' or 'topic neutral'.

An argument rather similar to the above rests on a different confusion. If we take the example of the after-image it will be objected that the after-image is patently not in physical space as the orange is but in some sort of psychological space. This objection falls down because I am not arguing that the after-image is a brain process. On my view there are no such entities as after-images, but there are processes of having-an-after-image. (These will be brain processes similar to those which go on in veridical seeing, but differing from them in being internally, not externally, stimulated.) I am arguing that the experience of having an after-image is in fact a brain process, and hence is in physical space. Similarly, if it is pointed out that the after-image is yellowish-orange I shall reply that the same fallacy is being committed. It is the experience of having the after-image that is the brain process, and this is not yellowish-orange. If you like you can say that the after-image is yellowish-orange, but this is only to say that the experience of having it is like the experience of seeing a physical object which really is yellowish-orange.

It may, however, be argued that a movement of electric charges in the brain can be swift or slow, straight or circular while an experience cannot be such. Now of course it is vastly to oversimplify what goes on in the brain to say that it can be swift or slow, straight or circular. The brain processes in which we are interested must be extraordinarily complex. Nevertheless, this does not touch the philosophical point of the objection. So let us concede for the sake of argument that the brain processes in question could be described as swift or slow, straight or circular. To rebut the objection I need only reply (analogously to my replies to objections in the previous two paragraphs) that if the premisses of the argument are correct and the brain process is swift or slow, straight or circular, then the experience *is* swift or slow, straight or circular. For on my view the experience is the brain process. The objection is correct in so far as it points out that in the introspective report the experience is not described as swift or slow, straight or circular. In the same way when I say 'somebody is coming through the garden' this

97

somebody is not described as my wife. But the somebody in question may very well *in fact* be my wife.

Jerome Shaffer, in the course of an acute article,* takes up a different position. Instead of saying, like me, that ordinary language leaves it open as to whether conscious experiences are somewhere or nowhere, he says that ordinary language implies that conscious experiences are *not* in physical space. He therefore argues that it is contrary to ordinary language to say that conscious experiences are brain processes. I am not sure how one decides between the hypothesis (*a*) that ordinary language ascribes *no* place to conscious states and (*b*) that it simply *leaves open* what place they are in, or indeed whether they are in any place at all. If, however, hypothesis (*a*) is accepted, then it must be admitted that I have not perfectly reconciled the brain process theory with ordinary language. To some extent ordinary language would have to be said to embody a dualistic metaphysics. Nevertheless, the switch in ordinary language to bring it in line with hypothesis (*b*) would be a very simple and painless one, involving hardly any readjustments to the rest of language. Indeed, I think that Shaffer admits as much, when in the second part of the article he in effect defends the brain-process theory against 'ordinary language' critics, when he considers the possibility of conceptual readjustment of ordinary language in the light of future physiological knowledge. Here my difference from him, I think, lies in the fact that, on account of the considerations of philosophical plausibility foreshadowed in Chapter I and developed in Chapters III and IV, I believe that it is reasonable to advocate this conceptual revision (if it is a revision) even in the light of present scientific knowledge.

Indeed, it may be precisely because our words mean what they *do* mean that we may come to *change* some of our locutions, *e.g.* to locate consciousness in the brain, not as a matter of metaphysical theory, as in this chapter, but as a matter of course, as common sense. Hilary Putnam,† influenced by Paul Ziff,‡ points out that a new way of talking may arise *because* of the old standard use of the words in question: a change in the conceptual context in which these words are used may indeed almost *force* a change in language

* 'Could Mental States be Brain Processes?' *Journal of Philosophy*, Vol. 58, 1961, pp. 813–22.

† In the article cited in footnote to page 92.

‡ See his *Semantical Analysis* (Cornell University Press, 1960).

habits. This is very different from arbitrarily *giving* a new use to a word.

We must now pass on to consider another objection.* This is that our experiences are private, immediately known only to ourselves, whereas brain processes are public, observable (in principle) by any number of external observers. If someone sincerely says that he is having a certain experience, then no one can contradict him. But if the physiologist reports something in the brain, then it is always *in principle* possible to say: 'Perhaps you are mistaken; you may be having an illusion or hallucination or something of the sort.' It will be remembered that I suggested that in reporting sensations we are in fact reporting likenesses and unlikenesses of brain processes. Now it may be objected (as has been done by K. E. M. Baier): 'Suppose that you had some electro-encephalograph fixed to your brain, and you observed that, according to the electro-encephalograph, you did *not* have the sort of brain process that normally goes on when you have a yellow sense datum. Nevertheless, if you had a yellow sense datum you would not give up the proposition that you had such a sense datum, no matter *what* the encephalograph said.' This part of the objection can be easily answered. I simply reply that the brain-process theory was put forward as a factual identification, not as a logically necessary one. I can therefore agree that it is logically possible that the electro-encephalograph experiment should turn out as envisaged in the objection, but I can still believe *that this will never in fact happen*. If it did happen I should doubtless give up the brain-process theory (though later I might come to doubt the correctness of my memory of the experiment and thus reinstate the theory!). Of course if the experiment were done on someone else I might simply doubt the sincerity of his sensation report. My acute critic has, of course, for this very reason fastened on the case where I have the electro-encephalograph fastened to my own head.

I have replied to this objection by granting to my critic the absolute incorrigibility of first-person sensation reports. That is, I have granted that reports of immediate experience differ from all other reports in that they have a 'private logic'. By this is meant that if a person (*a*) knows the language and (*b*) is sincere, is not lying, then as a matter of logic he *must* have the immediate ex-

* See the note by Kurt Baier mentioned in footnote to page 92.

perience that he reports. There is no logical room for error or mistake here. I can, I have said, grant all this and still reply to the objection as I did in the last paragraph. It should be noticed that I need not deny that sensation reports can have a different *logic* from the material object language of the physiologist. Many philosophers are willing to say that 'nation' talk 'has a different logic' from 'citizen' talk, and yet do not want to hold that nations are entities over and above citizens.

In spite of all this I wish nevertheless to move from defence to offence. There seems to me something extremely puzzling about the notion of absolute incorrigibility. It is alleged that it is logically impossible for someone sincerely to report a yellow after-image, say, and yet not have the yellow after-image. There is a difficulty here which is as much one for the dualist (and indeed for most behaviourists) as it is for the materialist. This is not surprising, because surely you cannot get rid of logical puzzles by shifting them to the realm of the ghostly. The difficulty is as follows. Very nearly the same argument has been independently produced by D. M. Armstrong and also by B. H. Medlin, as I found in correspondence with them.*

Both the materialist and the dualist will want to say that the sincere reporting of a sensation is one thing and the sensation reported is another thing. (So also will any behaviourist who analyses a pain into any behaviour other than the mere saying 'I have a pain'.) Now we have learned from Hume that what is distinguishable is separable. In other words, it must be logically possible that someone should sincerely report an experience and yet that the experience should not occur.

There is certainly something surprising about this conclusion,

---

* Since this book first went to press I have noticed a very similar argument by A. J. Ayer on p. 57 of his lecture 'Privacy', *Proceedings of the British Academy*, Vol. 45, 1959, pp. 43–65. There is a hint of a similar argument, though in a reversed form, in Norman Malcolm's discussion of Wittgenstein's *Philosophical Investigations*, in the *Philosophical Review*, Vol. 63, on p. 556, lines 13–14. This in effect argues from the incorrigibility of sensation reports to the untenability of Strawson's view about sensations. I think, however, that it can also be turned against Wittgenstein as interpreted by Malcolm. The argument is also similar to one used by A. I. Melden on p. 482 of his article 'Willing', *Philosophical Review*, Vol. 69, 1960, against the view that volitions are causes of actions. (See discussion of this by Kurt Baier in his article 'Pains', *Australasian Journal of Philosophy*, Vol. 40, 1962, pp. 1–23.)

but how can we avoid it? It is no good saying* that contingently connected things can be described by logically connected terms. Thus, it is contingent that Tom is the son of Harry, but logically impossible for a son not to have a father. This manoeuvre will not help us here. We could indeed make it a criterion of the sincerity of sensation reports that such reports should be true. This does not make a difference between reports of publicly observable events and reports of immediate experience. We could equally well, if we wished, make it a criterion of the 'sincerity' of a report of a traffic accident that a traffic accident occurred. In this case would we have conferred absolute incorrigibility on reports of traffic accidents?

Suppose someone says that you can imagine yourself being turned to stone, and yet having images, aches, pains, and so on. The reply should now be clear. You can imagine that the electrical theory of lightning is false. You can imagine that the evening star is not the morning star. You can imagine that the author of *Waverley* was not the author of *Ivanhoe*. Nevertheless, in fact lightning *is* an electric discharge, the evening star *is* the morning star, and the author of *Waverley* *was* the author of *Ivanhoe*. But then it may be said † 'what can be composed of nothing cannot be composed of anything'. The argument goes on as follows. The brain-process hypothesis is that there is a *contingent* identity between experiences and brain processes. Were the scientific facts otherwise we might have had to identify experiences with heart processes or liver processes, for example. But the 'turned to stone' argument suggests that there might have been no brain process, no heart process, no process of any sort.

The reply here is that the man who imagines himself being turned to stone surely *is* supposing that the experience is 'composed of something'. Certainly not of brain stuff, heart stuff, liver stuff, or any sort of bodily stuff, but surely he is then supposing that it is composed of some sort of non-physical ghost stuff. This is a possible hypothesis to set against mine. I argue for mine on the grounds of Occam's razor and scientific plausibility. To suggest that another hypothesis is logically possible is not to

---

* As Baier has done, in a different connection, in his article on 'Pains' mentioned in the previous footnote.

† As by my colleague, C. B. Martin. Martin would no longer argue in this way, however.

knock mine down *a priori*. Someone may now ask me what sort of brain process it is that I identify with experiences. It cannot be *any* sort of brain process, for there are brain processes which occur in dreamless sleep.

There are certainly many sorts of brain process that can at once be ruled out from consideration. Obviously we can rule out those that belong to the autonomic nervous system, which regulates such bodily functions as breathing. Only asthmatics and the like are conscious of their breathing. In an earlier paper I suggested that the difference between those brain processes, which according to me are experiences, and those which are not, may in part be the difference between what D. M. MacKay* has called *per*ception and what he has called *re*ception. Consider a robot which is designed to be able to learn to run along an irregular zigzag road. There are two ways in which this might be achieved, one more efficient than the other. The less efficient way would be as follows. There would be a negative feed-back mechanism which would act so as to minimise the angle between the direction in which the robot was travelling and the direction of the road in front of it. This would be an instance of *reception*. But suppose that after one or two trials of this sort it was able, by a learning mechanism, to incorporate within itself an active 'matching process', approximately isomorphic with the time pattern of zigs and zags in the road, and that this matching process determined the robot's own zigs and zags. Then suppose a negative feed-back mechanism which minimised the difference between the pattern of zigs and zags and the pattern of the matching process. By this means the robot could learn to traverse the route with far more efficiency (*e.g.* by going sharply round the bends rather than taking a wider circuit). A robot with an active matching process provides an instance of what MacKay terms *per*ception. If MacKay is right, what we ordinarily call 'perception' is perception in his sense, not reception. The suggestion that the only sorts of brain processes which are experiences are those of the perceptual sort does not work, however. For sometimes we unconsciously perceive something. Consider a case where we pick out a handkerchief from a drawer containing an assortment of clothes, without consciously realising that we have done so. This must involve

---

* D. M. MacKay, 'Towards an Information-flow Model of Human Behaviour', *British Journal of Psychology*, Vol. 47, 1956, pp. 30–43.

perception, rather than reception, in MacKay's sense. Maybe the distinction between perception and reception is part of the story, but it cannot be the whole story.

However, unsatisfactory though our knowledge may be, there is something we *can* say about the sorts of brain process which are conscious experiences. They are those which can be (though they are not always in fact) causal conditions of our uttering those introspective reports which we classify as reports of immediate experience.

It has been an essential part of my defence of the brain-process thesis that our reports of inner experiences are topic neutral in a certain way: that they report inner experiences essentially as 'like what goes on in me when . . .'. There are two respects in which reports of inner experiences go beyond this, but in neither case do these affect their topic neutrality.

In the first place we certainly can say that a pain, for example, waxes and wanes, becomes more or less intense. This is quite consistent with my theory, for terms such as 'wax' and 'wane' are topic neutral. They are equally applicable to brain processes and purely 'psychic' processes. They do not prejudice the case either way: in themselves they favour neither the brain process theory nor the dualistic theory.

In the second place we can characterise a pain, for example, as 'in my right thumb' or 'under my breast bone'. What is meant by this? It is quite clearly not that my pain is in my thumb or under my breast bone in the literal sense in which an abscess can be there. This is obvious when we consider that I might have a pain 'in my thumb' even though my thumb had been amputated. Moreover, I can be mistaken about where my abscess is in a way in which I cannot be mistaken about where my pain is. If I sincerely say that I have a pain in my thumb this is where the pain is. It is true that there may be nothing wrong with my thumb, and that the trouble is some inflammation in my upper arm. That does not in the least affect the correctness of my saying that the pain is in my thumb. Indeed, if I suspect that the pain in my thumb is due to some neuritis in my upper arm, and then say that my pain is in my upper arm, I shall quite mislead the doctor. (He may start looking for trouble in my shoulder, perhaps!) The philosophically interesting question is: 'What justifies me in localising a pain in my thumb?' A suggestion might be this: there is a one–one correlation between parts of the body touched and certain possible unanalysable *qualia* of the corresponding sensations. By experience we learn to correlate these *qualia* with the relevant parts of the body. The *qualia* would act as so-called 'local signs' of the parts of the body 'in' which the pain occurs. An alternative theory might replace these *qualia* by separate visual or tactual images of relevant parts of the body. (This was roughly Lotze's theory.) I reject these accounts. In particular, I see no need to suppose *qualia* as local signs. Nor do I suppose that we need to learn how to localise pains, *e.g.* by observing the tin-tack in the finger when I feel a certain pain. It may be that there is an inborn tendency to relate bodily sensations to parts of the body. This is a question for the psychologist. There need be no criterion which justifies us in locating bodily sensations. We may just locate them immediately. There seems to be no reason why there should not be some cerebral mechanism which associates the pains that come from point *A* of the body with the cerebral mechanism involved in, for example, perception and kinaesthesis of point *A*. There may just be a tendency to move point *A*, to direct our eyes towards *A*, and so on. To say that the pain is 'in' point *A* is just to give *expression* to these tendencies. Indeed, for those who have acquired language, one of these tendencies may just be to say to oneself 'in my thumb', or whatever it may be. The pain may 'touch off' the words.*

On the above account, the sense in which a pain can be 'in my thumb' is essentially neutral between a brain-process theory and traditional dualism. (Where I have supposed a cerebral mechanism associating brain processes with tendencies to point, touch, look at, or imagine, the dualist will suppose a psychic mechanism.) Thus, though such properties of pain as waxing and waning

---

* *Cf.* E. B. Titchener, *A Textbook of Psychology*, Part II, quoted by G. N. A. Vesey in his paper 'The Location of Bodily Sensations , *Mind*, Vol. 70, 1961, pp. 25–35. Vesey here criticises various forms of the local-sign theory. I agree with Vesey that it is clearly unnecessary for the local sign to be some associated imagery, nor need there by any learning process whereby some imagery comes to be associated with a sensation. There may simply be a neural mechanism which constitutes a causal inter-connection between the brain process which is the sensation and the brain process or state which explains the set of tendencies to look at, touch, or mention a certain part of the body. For this reason I see no need to accept Vesey's 'Sartre-type' account of the location of bodily sensations: indeed, I am not sure that I understand it.

and of being in my thumb are not properties of 'being like what goes on in me when . . .' they are equally 'topic neutral'. Whether there are any other sorts of introspectible properties of immediate experiences I do not know, but if there are, then, if I am right, they will share this 'openness' and 'topic neutrality'. In which case they will not provide an argument against the brain-process theory. It is incumbent on anyone who wishes to dispute the brain-process theory to produce experiences which are known to possess irreducibly 'psychic' properties, not merely 'topic neutral' ones. So far I do not think that anyone has done so.

If the brain-process theory is correct, then it is in principle possible that an appropriately constructed robot might be conscious, *i.e.* have sensations. If in its (perhaps electronic) brain there were the right sort of processes, analogous to those that go on in us when we are conscious, then this robot would be conscious too. In effect, we have cleared away one difficulty which people have felt about the idea of man as a physical mechanism. There are, however, other difficulties to be considered. These will be discussed in the next chapter.

VI

MAN AS A
PHYSICAL MECHANISM

DESCARTES thought that while animals were mere machines, men were machines with souls. As Ryle has put it,* according to Descartes man is a ghost in a machine. At first sight the mere fact of consciousness seems to prove Descartes' point. For it would seem that however complicated we made an electronic computer, for example, it would not be conscious. It would appear therefore that man differs from a physical mechanism in some very fundamental way. However, if my conclusions in the last chapter are correct these appearances are deceptive. There would seem to be no reason why a sufficiently complex electronic gadget should not be conscious or have experiences. If consciousness is a brain process, then presumably it could also be an electronic process. Provided the electronic process were of the same pattern as the appropriate neural process, it also would be a conscious experience.

According to Ryle, Descartes is wrong on another count as well. Not only is it incorrect to think of man as a ghost in a machine, it is also incorrect to think of man as a machine at all, even a ghostless one. I think that Ryle must here be thinking of rather simple mechanisms: the reasons he gives for saying that we are not machines turn on the peculiar purposefulness, appropriateness, and adaptiveness of human, and indeed animal, behaviour. To say that we have a mind is to say that we behave intelligently, not that

* Ryle, *op. cit.*
106

we have a soul or 'ghost'. But is there any reason why a machine should not have the sort of purposefulness, appropriateness, and adaptiveness that is characteristic of human beings? I shall contend that we have no reason for thinking that a machine could not have the human sort of intelligence, and therefore that the antecedent scientific plausibility of physicalism should lead us to espouse the view that men are physical mechanisms. The hypothesis that I shall put forward is an old one in that it goes back at least to La Mettrie's *L'Homme Machine*,* but it has been enormously strengthened by recent developments in cybernetics, the theory of self-regulating mechanisms. Let us therefore look with a critical eye at some of the arguments which have been brought up against the mechanistic theory of man.

MECHANISMS AND MACHINES

My thesis is that man is a physical mechanism, and I frequently express this loosely in the form 'man is a machine'. It is clearly useful to use the word 'machine' in this wide sense of 'physical mechanism': this use of the word has respectable ancestry, as is testified to by the phrases 'l'homme machine' and 'the ghost in the machine' which were quoted on the last page. It is nevertheless important to remember that this is not the colloquial use of the word 'machine'. It is not even the case that all of the artefacts which are mechanisms are (in the colloquial sense) 'machines'. It is not normal to call a watch, a telescope, a wireless set, or a howitzer a machine. Looms and printing presses are clearly machines, and so, of course, are such things as mowing machines, sewing machines, and milking machines. What is the difference between those artificial mechanisms which we call 'machines' and those which we do not call 'machines'? It is not that the machines are mechanical, full of cog wheels and the like, while the others are not. A watch has cog wheels, but it is not a machine but an instrument. A calculating machine may be purely electronic, and yet it is indubitably a machine. I suggest that we tend to call a thing a machine if it replaces men, or possibly animals, in the performance of some function. Indeed, a similar definition of

* J. O. de La Mettrie, *L'Homme Machine*, critical edition with an introductory monograph and notes by A. Vartanian (Princeton University Press, Princeton, N.J., 1960).

'machine' has been given by Louis Couffignal in his book *Les Machines à Penser*,* though I think as a stipulative definition rather than as an analysis of colloquial language. The loom replaces the hand weaver, the printing press replaces the scribe, the mowing machine replaces the man with the scythe, and the milking machine takes over the job of milking the cows. On the other hand, clocks, watches, wireless sets, and telescopes do not do better what was previously done by human beings. The wireless set, for example, has a function, but it does not replace a human being in the way in which the milking machine replaces the milkmaid. An interesting case is that of the gramophone. Normally it is not usual to call gramophones 'machines', but in some quarters where the gramophone is used in lieu of a dance band it is beginning to be called a 'record machine'. Notice also how an aeroplane used to be called 'a flying machine'. This was in the days when flying was a sport rather like hunting, and the aeroplane was a sort of mechanical flying horse. Now that the aeroplane is no longer a substitute for a horse, but is a conveyance like a bus, a train, or a lorry, it is no longer called 'a flying machine' but 'a craft'. A borderline case between machines and non-machines is that of machine guns and machine tools. These are not naturally called 'machines' *simplicitur* because they require not just an operator but a soldier or craftsman who exercises skill by means of them. (Like the man with the scythe rather than like the man with the mowing machine.) But a fully automatic lathe would, I imagine, come to be called 'a machine' purely and simply.

If this is right, then, that the colloquial meaning of the word 'machine' is 'that which replaces a man or an animal in the exercise of a function', we can see that there can be something absurd in saying that men are machines. It would be absurd to say that men are artefacts which do well or quickly tasks which were previously done badly or slowly by men. This, however, is in the colloquial sense of the word 'machine'. If we mean by 'machine' simply 'physical mechanism', then it is by no means obviously absurd to say that men are machines. The human brain has sometimes been compared to an electronic computer. Now computers are machines in the colloquial sense of the word: they are artefacts

* Les Editions de Minuit, Paris, 1952. Couffignal says: 'Nous désignons du nom de *machine* tout ensemble . . . capable de remplacer l'homme dans l'éxecution d'un ensemble d'opérations . . . proposé par l'homme' (p. 10).

which replace clerks and human calculators. They replace men in *some* of the activities which men perform. It is not surprising, therefore, that men are in many respects unlike computers. This does not prove, however, that an artefact could not be made to perform all the functions, both computational and non-computational, which men perform. Later on in this chapter we shall discuss the possibility of our one day being able to build machines which possess mathematical ingenuity. These might naturally come to be called 'thinking machines': they would replace the mathematician rather than the mere calculator. Such an artefact would nevertheless not replace men in *all* the functions which they perform. It should therefore not be surprising that it would not be in all respects like a man. This, however, will not go against the view that men are machines in the non-colloquial sense of 'physical mechanism'. Nor is it inconsistent with the supposition that it might one day be possible, though somewhat pointless, to build an artefact which behaved in every way just like a man.

The distinction between the colloquial sense of 'machine' as 'artefact made to perform some human function' and the wider sense of 'physical mechanism' allows us to deal with some criticisms of the cybernetic view of man. Thus, Mario Bunge, in a very acute book,* has pointed out that a computing machine no more performs artificial thinking than a motor car performs artificial walking. W. Mays† has said that calculating machines 'think by proxy'. Now of course a calculating machine does whatever it does (I would rather say 'calculate' than 'think') 'by proxy', and it is like a motor car in that it does a job *for us*. But this does not affect the question of whether some other sort of artefact could think not by proxy but on its own account. There seem to be two different reasons for saying that artefacts could not think. One is that they would lack consciousness. However, if the results of the last chapter are accepted, then it is possible that an artefact could be built which would possess consciousness. The other reason for saying that machines could not think is that they could not possess ingenuity: calculating is something done according to a routine which can be completely programmed into a machine. A good

---

* Mario Bunge, *Metascientific Queries* (Charles C. Thomas, Springfield, Illinois, 1959, p. 147).

† W. Mays, 'The Hypothesis of Cybernetics', *British Journal for the Philosophy of Science*, Vol. 2, 1951, pp. 249–50.

human calculator can indeed calculate without thinking what he is doing, just as he may walk to his office without thinking what he is doing. (A bad calculator may have to think, even when doing something even as routine as calculating.) Since calculating can be done without thought, it is not surprising that calculating machines do not think. What about a machine which was able to exercise ingenuity? We shall investigate shortly whether it is possible that we should one day be able to build machines which possess ingenuity.

However ingenious a machine was, in other words however much we were able to turn over to it non-routine problems which baffled us, it might still be said that such a machine would be essentially different from a man. Such a machine would just be a physical mechanism, and it has been common in recent philosophy to stress the fact that not all questions are physical questions. For example, it has been pointed out that to sign a document is not just to make certain physical *movements*. A machine could make exactly the same movements as I do in signing my name, and yet would not have signed anything. Nor would it make any difference if the machine made exactly the same movements as I do in writing *its* name, supposing it had a name. The machine would still not have signed anything. We may concede the point at once. Many of our concepts, such as those of a signature, are clearly not physical concepts but legal or sociological ones. An isolated machine could not sign a document, because the notion of signing presupposes a set of legal and sociological rules. Before a machine could sign a document it would have to belong to a society of machines. Suppose, however, that there were a group of machines which were able to communicate with one another, for example by beams of light detected by photo-electric cells. Suppose also that these machines were so complex that they had evolved, or perhaps had built in to them, a set of rules of behaviour and a legal and moral terminology whereby they controlled one another's behaviour. Such machines could correctly be said to sign documents. Some of the questions which these machines might ask one another, such as whether a document had been correctly signed, would not be physical questions but legal ones. No doubt, for the machines to be able to work within a legal system, they would have to be responsible agents, that is, capable of perception, of thinking, of memory, and understanding. To assert dogmatically that a machine is not capable of all of these is simply to beg the issues in question in this chapter and in the previous chapter. It is not at all necessary for me to accept the view that signing is analysable wholly in terms of physical movements of the hand. The right things would have to go on in the central nervous system or the electronic 'brain', and the right sort of legal or quasi-legal conventions would have to be in existence. The machines would be machines none the less. The remark, therefore, that not all questions are physical questions is irrelevant to the problem of whether men are or are not machines, in the sense of physical mechanisms. This should not surprise us. How many philosophical mechanists, even those of the crude nineteenth-century variety, would have wished to say that legal questions are physical questions?

PROBLEM-SOLVING INGENUITY

We must now consider in what way it might be possible to build ingenuity into a machine. One particularly instructive type of ingenuity is the problem-solving ingenuity required in mathematics. Some mathematical questions, such as a problem in long division, can be answered in a routine way, without the need for ingenuity. For such problems we have an algorithm or set of rules, which always tells us what to do next. Algorithms can be programmed into computing machines. The application of an algorithm can be very tedious for human beings, and moreover, a machine, because of its colossal speed of operations, is able to answer questions which it would take years, or even more than a lifetime, for human beings to answer. There are, however, problems in mathematics for which there are no algorithms. Indeed, it can be proved for certain mathematical theories that not only has no algorithm or 'decision procedure' been discovered for them but that there is none to be discovered. Logicians used to have to use ingenuity to prove theorems in the propositional calculus, but later it was discovered that an algorithmic method, namely the method of the truth tables, enabled us to check in a purely routine way whether or not a proposition was a theorem of the propositional calculus. Might the same thing one day happen in interesting branches of mathematics? It has been proved that this is not so. For these branches of mathematics no decision procedure will ever be found. Alonzo Church proved that even for the predicate calculus in logic there could be no decision procedure.* A machine which proved theorems in such a theory would certainly possess what in human beings we call ingenuity. Moreover, it would be natural, if we had such a machine, to call it a thinking machine. In a very real sense it would do our thinking for us, just as a milking machine milks our cows for us. Such a thinking machine would possess originality of the sort we ascribe to bright students or research workers, who have the knack of solving mathematical problems, though it would fall far short of the sort of creativeness possessed by men who create new branches of mathematics.

To fix our ideas, let us consider the possibility of making a machine which would be able to prove Fermat's last theorem, if indeed this theorem is provable. The case is peculiarly instructive, because at present we do not know whether the theorem *is* provable, or even whether it is true. It is also instructive because in spite of the difficulty, or perhaps impossibility, of proving it the proposition is very easy to state and to understand. It is a proposition of elementary number theory, the theory of the natural numbers $0, 1, 2, 3, \ldots$. The theorem is to the effect if x, y, z are integers and if n is an integer greater than 2, it is never the case that $x^n + y^n = z^n$. No integers for which $x^n + y^n = z^n$ and $n > 2$ have in fact been discovered, and most mathematicians would be prepared to guess that the theorem is in fact true. However, no proof of the theorem has ever been found, unless possibly by Fermat, the great seventeenth-century mathematician who conjectured the proof. He asserted in the margin of a book he had been reading that he had discovered a proof, but died without having disclosed the proof. Let us suppose that Fermat's theorem is true, and let us, furthermore, suppose for the sake of simplicity that there is a proof of it expressible entirely within elementary number theory. (It might, of course, turn out to be provable, but provable only within a wider system, such as the theory of the real numbers, even though it itself is a proposition expressible in elementary number theory. But let us for the present purposes suppose that there is a proof using only concepts of elementary number theory.) On these assumptions there is indeed a sense in which it is possible that a computer should discover the proof. Consider a rigidly

* For a survey of such questions see Martin Davis, *Computability and Unsolvability* (McGraw-Hill, New York, 1958).

formalised system of elementary number theory. It would be possible to programme a computer so that it could check whether a given string of symbols constituted a sequence of well-formed sentences of the formalised system, and if it did whether it constituted a proof of Fermat's last theorem. This corresponds to the familiar fact that it is a routine matter to check whether a putative proof is a proof or not, whereas it is not a routine matter to discover such a proof.

The machine could now be set to check all sequences of symbols of length one (*i.e.* of one symbol only), then all sequences of length two, then all sequences of length three, and so on. (We can suppose all sequences of equal length to be ordered lexicographically.) If there is a proof within elementary number theory of Fermat's last theorem the machine will eventually come to it. On the other hand, if there is no proof the machine will go on for ever and we shall never know whether this is because there is no proof or whether it is because the machine has not gone on for long enough. We might try to get over this by programming the machine to test each string of symbols for being either a proof or a disproof. Even so, there might remain the possibility that the theorem is neither provable nor disprovable. Nevertheless, the human mathematician would be in as bad a fix, wondering whether he should give up his quest.

The above method of searching for the proof will, as I said, ultimately produce the proof if there is a proof to be found. But it is necessary to point out that this is so only for an idealised machine given infinite time to play with. No actual machine can keep going indefinitely: it will wear out. Moreover, we want to get a proof in a reasonable time: even the next million years is too long for us. It should be clear that ingenious human mathematicians must get their proofs by a very different method from our machine. Suppose that the alphabet in which we express elementary number theory contains 10 symbols. Then in order to test all sequences of symbols 1000 symbols long the machine would have to test 10^{1000} sequences, which would take even the fastest electronic computer far longer than the whole past history of the universe (5×10^9 years) according to one plausible cosmological hypothesis. Of course it is true that the above procedure could be drastically shortened. In many cases, for example, the machine would have to examine only one or two symbols of a sequence to rule out the possibility of the sequence constituting a sequence of well-formed sentences (and hence of constituting a proof of the theorem). Nevertheless, even with such drastic short cuts built in, it is probable that any such machine would take an impracticably long time by human standards.

How does the human problem solver do his job? The psychology of mathematical inventiveness is a little-understood subject: advances in the psychology of thinking and in the mechanisation of thought processes are likely to come about through mutual influences between these subjects. But one obvious suggestion comes to mind. The mathematician who is casting about, trying to find the proof of some theorem, is likely to use strategies of proof which have worked in the past and to try small variations on them. To do this he must be able to recognise patterns and symmetries in formulae. Sometimes, for example, a tentatively chosen expression (say as a possible true lemma which may, if it can be proved, serve as a step towards the theorem to be proved) will be replaced by a more symmetrical or otherwise 'pretty' looking one. It is not out of the question that a machine should be built to do all of these things.* Computers can already be programmed so as to learn from their mistakes. The problem of devising mechanical methods of shape recognition has in great part been solved, and so there seems no reason in principle why a machine should not be able to look out for, and profit from, symmetry and other *gestalt* properties of symbolic expressions. If the reader objects to the words 'recognition' and 'look out for' on the ground that these imply consciousness, let him for the moment replace them by suitable behaviouristic equivalents. The problem of consciousness is not at issue in the present argument, though I should remind the reader that if the last chapter is on the right lines it should be possible, though unnecessary, to build consciousness into a machine. The problem of consciousness will be taken up again later in this chapter.

We may hope, then, that one day, by making use of abilities to learn from previous experience, and hence the ability to develop

---

* For recent thinking in this sort of direction see Dr Marvin L. Minsky's article, 'Some methods of artificial intelligence and heuristic programming', National Physical Laboratory Symposium on *Mechanisation of Thought Processes* (Her Majesty's Stationary Office, London, 1959), Vol. 1, pp. 5–27. Many other papers and discussions in this symposium are also relevant to the present topic.

heuristic techniques, aided perhaps by the ability to recognise patterns and symmetries, we shall be able to construct a proof-finding machine. This machine, unlike the ordinarily programmed computer, would be non-moronic. It would possess abilities, which if found in a human being would be taken as evidence of intelligence and originality. Let us call the problem of designing such a machine the *ingenuity problem*. That we are at present very far from having solved the ingenuity problem is incontestable. Nevertheless, it is equally true to say that the progress we have made, and are likely to make, in this direction is far from negligible. There are certainly no cogent *a priori* arguments why the ingenuity problem should not be solvable. Philosophers in the past have been far too ready to say what could not be done. Not so long ago they frequently said that purposiveness could not be built into a machine, and yet nowadays purposive mechanisms are a common-place of engineering, for example in the field of self-guided missiles. In the 1920s the psychologist William McDougall used to pro-pound an animistic theory, the 'hormic theory', to account for all types of purposiveness and adaptiveness, whether in human beings or in animals.* I suggest that anyone who takes a similar attitude with regard to *ingenuity* may find himself looking equally foolish.

If the ingenuity problem comes to be solved we shall have a complete reply to one possible argument against the mechanistic theory of mind. This objection stems from Church's theorem in mathematical logic. Church's theorem is to the effect that there is no decision procedure or algorithm for deciding whether or not any given sentence of the predicate calculus is a theorem of that calculus. (For those readers who are unversed in logic, it does not matter for our present purposes what exactly the predicate calculus is. However, it is the most important part of logic, and with the addition of suitable axioms, *e.g.* for set theory, can be used to formalise any interesting mathematical theory.) A computing machine could indeed be programmed in such a way that it churned out theorems in the predicate calculus, and so, if it were given as much time as it wanted, it would eventually produce a proof of any given theorem of the predicate calculus. However, if a given sentence has not been churned out we do not know whether this is because the sentence is not a theorem or whether

* W. McDougall, *Outline of Psychology*, 13th ed. (Methuen, London, 1949), pp. 71–3.

it is simply because the machine has not come to it yet. The machine will therefore tell us whether a given sentence is a theorem, if it is one, but it will be unable to tell us that a sentence is not a theorem if it is not one. It is not possible to remedy this situation by adding on to our theorem churning machine another machine which churns out non-theorems. It can be proved, and is indeed a corollary of Church's theorem, that there could never be a non-theorem churning machine. This is in the very same sense that we could not square the circle. There is a demonstrable mathematical impossibility in the idea of a computer which simply churns out non-theorems of the predicate calculus. We can put this by saying that whereas the class of theorems of the predicate calculus is 'canonical', the class of non-theorems is not canonical.

Often we can be either completely or pretty well convinced that a sentence of the predicate calculus is not a theorem: we may either have disproved it or we may, despite much ingenuity, have failed to prove it. With the mere machine which churns out theorems we cannot be so convinced. Maybe the sentence in which we are interested will be churned out, but not for millions of years yet. Indeed, with the churning-out machine we might not get many proofs of interesting theorems within a reasonable stretch of time. But if the ingenuity problem could be solved for machines a machine could be in as good a position as we are for discovering theorems and non-theorems of the predicate calculus. That is, in many cases it might be able to discover interesting theorems and non-theorems in a reasonable period of time. And if it failed to prove a theorem in a reasonable period of time it could put out as a 'guess' that the theorem was not provable.

THE ARGUMENT FROM GÖDEL

Some writers, such as P. Rosenbloom,* J. G. Kemeny,† E. Nagel and J. R. Newman,‡ and, most recently, J. R. Lucas,§ have

* P. Rosenbloom, *Elements of Symbolic Logic* (Dover, New York, 1951), p. 208.

† J. G. Kemeny, *A Philosopher looks at Science* (Van Nostrand, Princeton, N.J., 1959), p. 224.

‡ E. Nagel and J. R. Newman, *Gödel's Proof* (Routledge and Kegan Paul, London, 1959), pp. 100–1.

§ J. R. Lucas, 'Minds, Machines and Gödel', *Philosophy*, Vol. 36, 1961, pp. 112–27.

argued that another famous theorem in mathematical logic, namely Gödel's theorem, shows, in a different way, that men are not machines. For short I shall call this argument 'the argument from Gödel'. It should be emphasised that this argument is a philosophical one based on Gödel's theorem, and I have no idea whether Gödel himself would wish to see his theorem used in this way. Gödel's theorem has an implication with respect to most parts of mathematics which is similar to that which Church's theorem has with respect to the predicate calculus, and the reply we must make is here similar to that which we made in the last paragraph. But Gödel's theorem raises, in the view of writers such as those who I have just mentioned, another difficulty. This objection goes as follows. Gödel has shown that for any formalisation of elementary number theory (the theory concerned only with the natural numbers 0, 1, 2, 3, etc.) there will be a sentence which is neither provable nor disprovable within the system. However, *we*, by means of an argument in the metalanguage, in which we talk not *with*, but *about*, the formal system, can show that this sentence is true. Thus, it would appear that no matter how many axioms and rules we programme into a computing machine there will always be some sentence which the human being can prove, but the machine cannot.

The solution of the ingenuity problem would not by itself enable us to get round the above difficulty. The solution of the ingenuity problem only enables us to design a machine which will probably do in some specified finite time a task which the moronic machine could certainly do if given infinite time, *i.e.* as much time as it needed. The argument from Gödel's theorem purports to show that there is something that we can do and which the moronic machine could not do even in infinite time. Equally, therefore, a non-moronic machine could not do it. The argument would seem to show, therefore, that we are not machines—not even non-moronic machines of the sort we envisaged when we considered the ingenuity problem.

The argument goes as follows. Consider some formal language L_0 adequate for elementary number theory. Gödel has shown that if L_0 is consistent then there is some closed arithmetical sentence*

* A closed arithmetical sentence is one without free variables. Thus 'for any x and any y, $x + y \geqslant x$' is a closed sentence of elementary number theory. '$x < 7$' is not a closed sentence. It contains the free variable 'x'. It

expressible in the symbolism of L_0 which cannot be proved or disproved in L_0. By reasoning which makes use of the syntax language of L_0, however, we can show that this proposition which is undecidable within L_0 is in fact true. (The syntax language of a language L is the language in which are expressed the axioms and rules of L. The syntax language could itself be axiomatised. In the present case 'semantics language' might be a better term than 'syntax language,' since the language must be able to define 'true'.) Though a computing machine T_0 can be specified which will prove or disprove all provable or disprovable sentences of L_0 it will not, even given infinite time, prove the Gödelian undecidable sentence of L_0, which nevertheless *we*, by ascent to the syntax language, can show to be true. Of course, by adjoining the syntax language of L_0 to L_0 we get a more powerful language L_1: corresponding to which there will be a machine T_1, which given infinite time could prove or disprove all the decidable propositions of L_1, including the already mentioned undecidable sentence of L_0. Nevertheless, there will similarly be some Gödelian undecidable proposition of L_1, which we can prove by ascending to the syntax language of L_1. And so on. It looks as though however far we go up the sequence of languages $L_0, L_1, L_2, \ldots$ and of the corresponding machines $T_0, T_1, T_2, \ldots$ there will always be some proposition which the machine cannot prove (even given infinite time) but which we can prove.

The rule for constructing the sequence of languages $L_0, L_1, L_2, \ldots$ could even be built into a machine. This would be a machine T_ω corresponding to a language L_ω. Nevertheless, in L_ω there would be an undecidable sentence provable only in a language $L_{1+\omega}$. The process could indeed be carried on through the constructible ordinals. So equally is it with the human being. We must note that any one of our languages must contain an axiom to the effect that the language next lower down the hierarchy is consistent. But what is our justification for adding such an axiom? Of course, you can bet your boots that elementary number theory is consistent, but betting your boots is not the same as proof. In the previous paragraph I have talked of 'prov-

---

is rather trivial that such sentences containing free variables are neither provable nor disprovable in elementary number theory. They do not express truths or falsehoods, though they are *true of* some numbers, *false of* others. '$x < 7$' is true of 6, false of 8. We can think of an open sentence as a predicate.

ing' the truth of the undecidable sentence of L_0 by ascending to the syntax language of L_0. But since such a proof would need such an axiom as 'that L_0 is consistent', it would be better to say simply that by an argument in the syntax language we 'convince ourselves' that the undecidable sentence is true. We are here concerned with something less than rigorous proof, for we do not know that arithmetic is consistent. I neglect here, however, the technical and controversial question of how much weight should be put on Gentzen's proof of the consistency of arithmetic, which makes use of so-called *transfinite* methods. It will not affect the goodness or badness of the solution to our problem which I propose in the next section.

AN INDUCTIVE MACHINE

If we became able to solve the ingenuity problem, discussed earlier in this chapter, we should be able to design a machine, which when programmed to prove and disprove propositions in a language L, could by observation of its own linguistic behaviour ascertain the syntactical and semantical rules of L. This ascertainment would, of course, be inductive in nature, and so would not be possessed of full mathematical rigour. (I am here using 'inductive' in the sense in which we contrast 'inductive' and 'deductive' logic, not in the sense of 'mathematical induction'.) However, in this respect the machine would be neither better nor worse off than a human being. It is true that in some cases the syntax and semantics of a language L_n is given in a language L_{n+1} in the form of explicit rules, but then the syntax and semantics of L_{n+1} must be known intuitively or given in the form of rules expressed in a language L_{n+2}, and so on. Sooner or later we must stop at a language whose rules are known 'intuitively', which means in fact that they have to be ascertained, perhaps unconsciously, by empirical observation of linguistic behaviour. This empirical ascertainment of the rules of language (whether in the human being or the machine) is, mathematically speaking, a bit of 'cheating', and this provides a way of getting round the argument from Gödel. Suppose that we have a machine programmed for a language L_0 and also with built into it a capacity to learn empirically such things as the rules of its own behaviour. By ascertaining the rules of its own language L_0 it can convert itself into an L_1 machine, and hence it can go on to ascertain the rules of L_1 and convert itself into an L_2 machine, and so it can go up the hierarchy of languages as long as the capacity of its storage units is not exhausted. Until this point is reached it can convert itself from an L_n machine to an L_{n+1} machine, so that it is then able to prove the Gödelian undecidable sentence of L_n. At any moment there will be true propositions which it cannot prove, but which it can prove at a later moment when it has converted itself to a machine of greater logical power. Ultimately it will exhaust its storage capacity, but equally the human being will also, literally, become exhausted.

This method of getting round the argument from Gödel seems to me to be a perfectly plausible one.* It depends on the possibility of machines which can learn from experience. It is admittedly beyond our present technological powers to make a machine of the sort required, but there does not seem to me to be any *a priori* or physical reason why such a machine should not exist.

CREATIVITY AND FREEDOM

Nothing that has been said so far bears on the question of whether a machine could be capable of the higher flights of mathematical creativity. Solution of the ingenuity problem would enable us, in theory at least, to design a problem-solving machine. Now a machine which was able to produce for us a proof of some well-known unproved theorem, such as Fermat's last theorem, would indeed do something which, if it were done by a human being, would be deserving of very high honour. Nevertheless, even this sort of feat would not be regarded by most mathematicians as comparable to that of inaugurating a new branch of mathematics, such as, for example, the Galois theory of equations or the theory of recursive functions. Those mathematicians who invent, or help to invent, such quite new branches of mathematics are possessed of a creativity of a very high order. Nevertheless, the mere fact that at present we do not know how to make a machine with creativity of this sort does not provide a very strong argument

* Since writing this I have noticed a hint in the same direction in F. H. George, *The Brain as a Computer* (London, Pergamon Press, 1961), p. 3, and in his *Cognition* (London, Methuen, 1962), p. 209.

that machines with this sort of creativity are impossible. After all, it is not so long since purposive mechanisms or machines which are capable of shape recognition, such as the new machines which can scan a printed page and feed the equivalent of the letters on it directly into a computer, would have seemed quite inconceivable. There are certainly no apparently knock-down arguments like the arguments from Church's theorem and from Gödel's theorem, and we have seen cause to reject these. Unless an argument is a cogent *a priori* one of this sort it seems to be no better than an appeal to our present technological ignorance. Its propounders may be no better based than those who denied the possibility of a heavier-than-air flying machine.

We must agree, nevertheless, that there is often much loose talk about computers.* As a reply to such loose talk, it may be said that a machine does not calculate: it is we who calculate by means of it. It is indeed a valid point that what we ordinarily call 'calculating' is: (*a*) something which we do consciously, and (*b*) something which is set in the context of our whole language and way of life. This certainly shows that our ordinary calculating machines do not really 'calculate', but it does not prove that a more complex machine, which was (*a*) conscious and (*b*) capable of subtle linguistic and inter-personal (or inter-machine) behaviour, could not properly be said to do so. Again, consider the notion of 'reading'. It is, in a sense, incorrect to say that existing 'reading machines' really read. Consider a machine which is able to scan a printed page and feed the sequence of letters on it into a computer in the form of series of electrical impulses. This is not truly a reading machine if the connotation of 'reading' includes that of 'understanding' or even 'consciousness'. But it would be doing that part of reading which is done by a person who reads a novel to a dim-sighted friend, yet so inattentively that he is not conscious of the words he is reading. Such a person would indeed be doing little more than converting the printed symbols into the appropriate sounds. (At any rate if the words were written in a phonetic alphabet: to build a machine which would do the same with ordinary written English would be more difficult.) The exaggerations of the cyberneticians who use psychological vocabulary in connection with computers and the like should not cause us to go to the opposite extreme and deny that such

* As pointed out by Bunge, *op. cit.*

psychological language could be perfectly properly applied to a sufficiently complex machine.

Sometimes it is felt that our alleged immediate intuition of freedom in action is incompatible with the idea of man as a machine. However, I see no absurdity in the conception of a machine which has free will. That is a machine might make use of the information at its disposal to compute what its next move should be, and might be made so as to put the result of this computation into execution Such a machine would do something equivalent to deliberation in any sense in which this concept is at all clear.

Why is it that we find it useful to distinguish some acts as 'free' and others as 'not free'? Consider a very simple case. Suppose young Tommy has not done his homework, and the teacher has to decide whether to punish him or not. It may be that Tommy has not done his homework because he is too stupid. Then there is no point in punishing him or blaming him. Caning a stupid boy does not make him less stupid. On the other hand, Tommy may not have done his homework because he was lazy. In this case the teacher might quite reasonably punish him. The threat of punishment can make a lazy boy less lazy. Similar considerations apply in the case of physical restraints. If a man does not come home to dinner on time because he gets stuck in a lift there is not much point in his wife expostulating with him. He will as a result be no more likely in future to extricate himself from incarceration. But if a man is late for dinner because he called at a bar, then there is some point in his wife's expostulation. Maybe it will tend to make him mend his ways. (Of course, if expostulation drives him all the more into bars, then it would equally be reasonable for the wife to cease her nagging!) Similar considerations explain why it may be reasonable to treat as not guilty those men who commit crimes as a result of some mental disease. If a man commits a crime because he is an extreme paranoiac, then there is little point in punishing him. Rational considerations, threats, and the like will not have the least effect on him, nor will his punishment have an effect (as an example) on other paranoiacs. Non-paranoiacs, of course, will not be reassured, because they will know that they have no such let-out themselves. A lot of the provisions in ordinary criminal law can be made intelligible in this sort of way. Perhaps not all can be, because law depends partly on tradition and common feeling, and so may not always be rationally justifiable.

In the above ways, then, we can make a perfectly sensible distinction between free and unfree actions, and this distinction is in great part co-extensive with that which is made in common life by unreflecting people. This distinction is by no means incompatible with determinism. It is because reasoning, persuasion, and threats can be causal factors in determining human behaviour that it is reasonable to reason, to persuade, and to threaten. Consider now an electronic machine which was so complex that it could be influenced by reason, persuasion, or threats. Such a machine might be deterministic. If it were, and if we could have complete knowledge of the characteristics of the machine and of the information being fed into it, we could predict what it would do.* Alternatively, we could conceive of an unpredictable machine. Suppose it contained a Geiger counter whereby it was able to pick up isolated chance effects on the quantum level, and that as a result its behaviour was partly undetermined. Such a machine would be like the human being according to those philosophers who have thought that the indeterminacy of quantum mechanics provided a loop-hole for free will in human beings. Such philosophers make several mistakes. The first is the mistake of supposing that the human brain is likely to be triggered off by effects on the quantum level. Even a single neuron is a huge macroscopic object by the standards of quantum mechanics, and furthermore, the failure to fire of an odd neuron is unlikely to affect behaviour. There is almost certainly a great deal of redundancy in the human brain, and any thought or action almost certainly depends on the mass behaviour of a large number of neurons.† This sort of redundancy is in fact, to a much lesser extent, built into certain computing machines, when it is necessary that they should work in a reliable way even though they have unreliable components.

If we think of the human brain as a machine it is plausible to think of it as a deterministic machine. Actually the operation of a deterministic machine could be quite indistinguishable from that

* Unless it is in strong interaction with us—in which case it would be influenced by our predictions, and interesting logical difficulties arise. See K. R. Popper, 'Indeterminism in Quantum Physics and in Classical Physics', *British Journal for the Philosophy of Science*, Vol. I, 1950–1, pp. 117–33 and 173–95. See also G. F. Dear, 'Determinism in Classical Physics', *ibid.*, Vol. II, 1960–1, pp. 289–304.

† As D. M. MacKay has pointed out in his talk 'Brain and Will', *Listener*, Vol. 57, 1957, pp. 788–9.

of an indeterministic machine. Consider first an indeterministic machine which behaved in one or another of two ways according to whether it did or did not pick up some indeterministic quantum effect for which the probability was $\frac{1}{2}$. Consider, secondly, an exactly similar machine, except that instead of having a device for picking up a quantum effect whose probability was $\frac{1}{2}$ it had a device for scanning a table of random numbers and that it behaved in one or another of two ways according to whether the number scanned was odd or even. The behaviour of the two machines would be quite indistinguishable.

If a machine is capable of making choices and of being influenced by punishment and reward, then it has in essence all that is needed for free will.

In the case of free actions, in the above sense, we say that a man 'could have' done otherwise. What does 'could have' mean here? There is admittedly a *possible* sense in which we might use the words 'could have', according to which a man, if he is a deterministic mechanism, could not have done otherwise than he in fact has done. This sense is that from a precise description of the initial conditions (the input to his sense organs and his present brain state) and of the mode of functioning of his nervous system, it could in principle be deduced what his immediate action would be. Indeed, if the universe as a whole were deterministic, then Laplace's superhuman calculator* could from a complete description of its state at time t_0 and from a knowledge of sufficient laws of nature predict what its state will be at any other time t_1. In this sense of 'could have' a man perhaps could never do other than he in fact does. But is this strained and metaphysical sense of 'could have' the one which is important when we ordinarily talk of free will, when we say that on some occasions a man could have done otherwise than he in fact did?

I suggest that in the contexts in which we ordinarily say that a man 'could have' or 'could not have done otherwise' we are using 'could have' in quite another sense. This other, common, non-metaphysical sense of 'could have' may be elucidated by means of the following example. Suppose that I drop an ink pot on to the floor. For some reason it does not break. I say: 'It did not break,

---

* Marquis P. S. de Laplace, *A Philosophical Essay on Probabilities*, translated from the 6th French edition by F. W. Truscott and F. L. Emory (Dover, New York, 1951), p. 4.

and what's more, it could have broken.' A stone, however, 'could not have broken'. What is the difference here? The difference is that within a very wide range of initial conditions I can predict that the stone will not break. Whether it falls on a sharp end or on a blunt face, whether it is dropped from two feet or ten feet, whether it is dropped with a spinning motion, or without a spinning motion, it still will not break. With the ink pot, in some cases it will break and in some cases it will not break. It may be that in some cases we are unable to predict whether it will break or not. It depends on what *exactly* the initial conditions are. Of course, a sufficiently knowledgeable and powerful calculator who knew the exact elasticity and strength of the glass of the ink pot, the exact velocity with which it leaves my hand as it is dropped, the exact distance to the ground, and so on, could perhaps in *every* case predict whether it will break or not. The words 'it could have broken' and 'it could not have broken' are useful simply because of our imprecise knowledge of initial conditions and of our limited powers of computation. In the case of the stone even we can predict that it will not break. Within a fairly wide margin of error, here, the initial conditions do not matter.

I suggest that the 'could have' in 'he could have done otherwise' is analogous to the 'could have' in 'the ink pot could have broken'. There is a slight qualification to be made to this. It is as natural to say that 'the ink pot *might* have broken' as it is to say that 'it *could* have broken'. But it is more natural to say that a criminal 'could have' behaved virtuously than it is to say simply that he 'might have' done so. The difference is, I suggest, as follows. The initial conditions which are unknown to us are of two sorts. In the first place, there are those which make up the external stimuli. In the second place there are those which specify a person's internal state. It is when our ability to predict, on the basis of a set of initial conditions, what a man will do, is due to unsureness about the *internal* initial conditions that we tend to say 'could have'. 'Could', unlike 'might', carries suggestions of the possibility of internal effort.* Whether the ink pot breaks or not depends on the precise motions with which we dropped it and the precise characteristics of the floor on which it falls. With 'he could have done otherwise' we are presupposing not only a range of

* See D. J. O'Connor, 'Possibility and Choice', *Aristotelian Society Supplementary Volume* 34, 1960, pp. 1–24, especially p. 19.

possible external initial conditions but also that the internal state of the man may vary from time to time. An additional uncertainty has crept in. But to admit this is in no way to say anything incompatible with the possibility that men are deterministic mechanisms.

One of the sorts of variable initial condition that may perhaps determine a man to do one action rather than another are social pressures such as threats and promises, praise and blame. This is why the question of whether or not a man 'could have done otherwise' is important in practical ethics and in criminal law. Once more we have nothing incompatible with the view of man as a deterministic machine.*

A special case of the view I have been concerned to refute, namely that determinism is incompatible with free will, is the contention that if determinism is true our assertions occur only because of *causes*, and not because they are based on *good reasons*. As a corollary it has sometimes been asserted that naturalism is self-refuting.† It has been argued that if a complete causal explanation of human behaviour were possible, then if this behaviour were a piece of so-called reasoning we should have no reason to accept its conclusion. For it is well known that when we find that someone has said something because he has been hypnotised to do so, or because he has a lesion in his brain, or because he is feeling liverish, we discount what he says. In short, when we are able to give a causal explanation of a person's verbal behaviour we regard it as irrational and we regard his conclusions as unfounded. Saying something because of causes therefore seems to be incompatible with saying something because of reasons. Now if naturalism were true the naturalist's own arguments would be determined by material causes in his brain, not by reasons. So if naturalism is true we have no reason to believe in the validity of the naturalist's argument that it is true, and the argument is therefore self-refuting.

---

* See R. E. Hobart, 'Free Will as Involving Determinism', *Mind*, Vol. 43, 1934, pp. 1–27.

† As by J. B. S. Haldane, *Possible Worlds* (Evergreen, London, 1940), p. 209, and by C. S. Lewis, *Miracles* (Bles, London, 1947), Chapter 3. But later repudiated by Haldane in 'I Repent an Error', *Literary Guide*, April 1954. For further criticism of the argument see A. G. N. Flew, 'The Third Maxim', *Rationalist Annual*, 1955, pp. 63–6. Further discussion by E. Gellner, 'Determinism and Validity', *ibid.*, 1957, pp. 68–79, Flew, 'Determinism and Validity Again', *ibid.*, 1958, pp. 39–51.

The fallacy in the above reasoning consists in the supposition that if a complete causal explanation of behaviour is possible, then that behaviour must be irrational, *i.e.* in the supposition that acting from causes and acting from reasons are mutually exclusive.

How do we decide whether an argument is based on *good reasons*? We apply various tests for validity. Thus, if a man says that most of the students in the university like sport and that most of them work hard, and that therefore most of the students both like sport and work hard, we refute him by pointing out that the inference does not hold, perhaps by citing an example of an inference which is of the same form and which has true premisses but a false conclusion. (For example: most of the positive integers less than ten are greater than four, and most of the positive integers less than ten are less than six, but it is not the case that most of the positive integers less than ten are both greater than four and less than six.) In refuting the man in this way we do not in the least concern ourselves with the causes or lack of causes of his making his inference.

Why, then, do we sometimes discount a person's remark because we can assign some cause for it, such as hypnotism, neurosis, a bad liver, or a lesion of the brain? It is surely because we have noticed that frequently these conditions are associated with irrationality. To have made this discovery we must have had *independent* criteria of rationality and irrationality. Presumably in a great many cases, when people do not have bad livers, brain lesions, neuroses, or post-hypnotic states, but have, it may be, red hair and freckles, they argue quite correctly. That is, we find no correlation between red hair and irrationality or between freckles and irrationality. Moreover, conditions such as hypnotism and brain lesions only lead us to *suspect* irrationality: however bad a man's brain lesion was or however much he had been hypnotised, if we checked his argument and found that it obeyed the laws of logic and had well-attested premisses we should have to pay as much attention to it as if it had been propounded by anyone else.

If determinism is true, then all arguments are caused. From this it follows that some causally determined arguments must be good arguments. For among these causally determined arguments must be some which have passed the independent tests for rationality. It follows that the argument that naturalism is self-refuting is not valid. This may forcibly be brought out by comparing correct deduction with correct computation. Consider an adding machine which is set to add 137 to 428. If it functions correctly it will produce the answer 565. But of course it may not function correctly. A tooth may be missing from a certain gear wheel, and in consequence it may produce the answer 555. A causal explanation of the failure will be quite easy. On the other hand, if we know the way in which the machine is constructed we can equally give a causal explanation of its success if no tooth is missing and it *does* produce the answer 565. If it were not for these causes it would not function correctly. Even if we do not have a full understanding of the working of a machine we may still suspect that it will function incorrectly if we find a tooth missing on a certain cog wheel. We may have observed in the past that machines with such a tooth missing have often given wrong answers. Similarly, we may have observed that the political prognostications of liverish men are frequently unreliable. This does not mean that there is not some causal explanation of the correct prognostications of normal men, any more than the fact that the missing tooth provides a causal explanation of the malfunctioning of the adding machine implies that there is no causal explanation of the correct functioning of a good adding machine. The moral for the argument that naturalism is self-refuting should be obvious.

When a mathematical logician theorises about computing machines he discusses idealised machines called Turing* machines. These could in principle be realised in a number of ways, either electronically or mechanically (with toothed wheels and so on) or even as a cardboard 'toy', or as human beings proceeding according to rigidly laid down rules. The actual 'hardware' or physical realisation is mathematically irrelevant. What matters is that there should be a number of states, a tape that can be scanned, and rules to the effect that if such and such a symbol is on the scanned part of the tape the machine proceeds to move to the right or left or stay put, to erase the symbol or print such and such a new one, and to change into a new state. The whole arithmetical notion of computability can be mirrored in terms of such machine states and machine instructions. Hilary Putnam has called machine states as

* After A. M. Turing. See his paper 'On Computable Numbers, with an Application to the Entscheidungsproblem', *Proceedings of the London Mathematical Society*, Ser. 2. Vol. 42, 1937, pp. 230–65; Correction, *ibid.*, Vol. 43, 1937, pp. 544–6.

thus abstractly defined 'logical states', and has suggested that old-fashioned introspective psychology was really an attempt to discover a theory of the mind in terms of logical states. These logical states are not non-physical or 'ghostly' states: they are abstractions from the physical and from the non-physical too. (Even immaterial souls could function as Turing machines.) The logical states are simply neutral between various possible realisations: the fact that we might discuss the mind in terms of such logical states no more implies that the mind is not a function of the physical than does the possibility of treating an electronic computer as though it were an abstract Turing machine imply that the computer is not a piece of solid hardware. Putnam interestingly suggests that introspective psychology did not fail, as has often been thought, because of methodological reasons: it failed for empirical reasons—as he says 'the mental states and "impressions" of human beings do not form a causally closed system to the extent to which the "configurations" of a Turing machine do'.* (It is hard to treat the human brain as a computer, partly because of its immense complexity, but mainly because of the continual stream of incoming 'information', so that its 'programme' is continually changing.)

The possibility of a 'logical description' of a computer does not confer a ghost on the computer. It is tempting to think that the mind–body problem is an outcome of the same sort of confusion as we would get if we confused the 'logical' and 'physical' descriptions of a computing machine. Nevertheless, there is the additional trouble of dealing with *consciousness*. I hope, however, that this was dealt with, with some approximation to satisfactoriness, in our previous chapter. In the following chapter we leave the problems of mind and matter for a rather different topic, that of space and time. Even here, however, we shall find concealed subjectivism and anthropocentricity rearing its head. Quite apart from this,

---

* Hilary Putnam, 'Minds and Machines', in Sidney Hook (ed.), *Dimensions of Mind* (New York, Collier, 1961), pp. 138–64. This also contains an elegant refutation, different from mine, of the argument from Gödel. My solution, though mathematically less satisfying, can perhaps be defended as being probably more closely related to the way in which the human brain actually works. A rather different argument, of the 'mathematical' sort, has been suggested to me by W. V. Quine. See the last paragraph of my paper 'Gödel's Theorem, Church's Theorem, and Mechanism', *Synthese*, Vol. 13, 1961, pp. 105–10.

however, the topic is an interesting one for a philosopher who wishes to understand man's place in the universe. I shall be advocating that we should think within a four-dimensional space–time framework. This has in fact been forced on physicists by the theory of relativity, but there are philosophical reasons for thinking in terms of space–time which are quite independent of relativity.

VII

THE SPACE–TIME WORLD

IN the Middle Ages the Aristotelian view that man stood at the centre of the cosmos prevailed. There was a spherical earth around which the various sublunary and superlunary spheres rotated. This cosmology was clearly very congenial to Christian theology. Even though the theologian admitted the existence of superior created intelligences, those of the angels, he still gave to man a unique place in the cosmos. According to him, the great theme of cosmic history was the fall and redemption of man, and it was God himself who took on human form. No wonder that there was resistance against the non-anthropocentric cosmologies of Copernicus and later scientists. Modern cosmology is even less anthropocentric. According to some modern cosmological hypotheses, there may be hundreds of thousands, or even millions, of inhabited planetary systems in our galaxy alone. It is likely that some of the inhabitants of some of these systems will be incomparably superior in intelligence to human beings. It would be an unlikely coincidence if we were the top dogs: indeed, it is quite improbable when we think of the millions of years of evolution before us, provided that we avoid blowing up our planet in the meantime. (Almost certainly life on some planets of remote stars will have got going long before life on ours did.) The view of man which was canvassed in the last chapter is corrective of an anthropocentric outlook: in regarding man as a physical mechanism we regard him as part of nature. It is so common in literary and popular thought to think of man not as part of nature but somehow as set over against it that a conscious effort to think of man as part of nature is very valuable. After a bit it becomes second nature to do so, and one gets a new and highly satisfying view of the world. Flying in the dark over the empty countryside, our aeroplane eventually comes down over the lights of a great city: how unnatural all this is, we feel, after so many miles of primeval bush and mountain. And then, we may reflect, it is not unnatural at all: birds make nests, but men make street lights and neon signs.

ANTHROPOCENTRICITY OF SOME TEMPORAL CONCEPTS

There is one feature of common ways of thinking which projects another sort of anthropocentric idea on to the universe at large. One can easily get the idea that the notions of past, present, and future apply objectively to the universe. In contrast, I shall argue that the concepts of past, present, and future have significance relative only to human thought and utterance and do not apply to the universe as such. They contain a hidden anthropocentricity. So also do tenses. On the other hand, the concepts of 'earlier', 'simultaneous', and 'later' are impeccably non-anthropocentric. I shall argue for a view of the world as a four-dimensional continuum of space–time entities, such that out of relation to particular human beings or other language users there is no distinction of 'past', 'present', and 'future'. Moreover, the notion of the flow of time is the result of similar confusions. Our notion of time as flowing, the transitory aspect of time as Broad has called it, is an illusion which prevents us seeing the world as it really is.

THE SPACE–TIME WORLD

A man or stone or star is commonly regarded as a three-dimensional object which nevertheless *endures* through time. This enduring through time clearly brings a fourth dimension into the matter, but this fact is obscured by our ordinary language. In our ordinary way of talking we stress the three-dimensionality of bodies, and by our notion of the permanent in change we conceal the fact that bodies extend through time. For philosophical reasons, therefore, it is of interest to discuss a way of talking which does not make use of the notion of the permanent in change. This explicitly four-dimensional way of talking has had important applications in physics. It needs, however, a bit of philosophical tidying up.

In what follows I shall want to make use of tenseless verbs. I shall indicate tenselessness by putting these verbs in italics. Tenseless verbs are familiar in logic and mathematics. When we say that two plus two *equals* four we do not mean that two plus two equals four at the present moment. Nor do we mean that two plus two always equalled four in the past, equals four now, and will always equal four in the future. This would imply that two plus two will equal four at midnight tonight, which has no clear sense. It could perhaps be taken to mean that if someone says 'two plus two *equals* four' at midnight tonight, then he will speak truly, but then 'at midnight tonight' does not occur in the proposition that is mentioned.

It is perfectly possible to think of things and processes as four-dimensional space–time entities. The instantaneous state of such a four-dimensional space–time solid will be a three-dimensional 'time slice'* of the four-dimensional solid. Then instead of talking of things or processes changing or not changing we can now talk of one time slice of a four-dimensional entity *being* different or not different from some other time slice. (Note the tenseless participle of the verb 'to be' in the last sentence.)

When we think four-dimensionally, therefore, we replace the notions of change and staying the same by the notions of the similarity or dissimilarity of time slices of four-dimensional solids. It may be objected that there is one sort of change which cannot be thus accommodated. For of any event, or of any time slice, it may be said on a certain occasion that it is in the future, and that later on it becomes present, and that later still it becomes past. It seems essential to say such things as that, for example, event E was future, is present, and will become past. The notion of change seems to be reintroduced into our four-dimensional scheme of things.

The objector is going too fast. If we are going to eliminate the notion of change we had better, to preserve consistency, eliminate also words such as 'past', 'present', 'future', and 'now'. Let us re-

---

* This vivid expression is used by J. H. Woodger. See his 'Technique of Theory Construction', *International Encyclopedia of Unified Science*, Vol. 2, No. 5 (University of Chicago Press, 1939).

place the words 'is past' by the words '*is* earlier than this utterance'. (Note the transition to the tenseless 'is'.) Similarly, let us replace 'is present' and 'now' by '*is* simultaneous with this utterance', and 'is future' by '*is* later than this utterance'. By 'utterance' here, I mean, in the case of spoken utterances the actual sounds that are uttered. In the case of written sentences (which extend through time) I mean the earliest time slices of such sentences (ink marks on paper). Notice that I am here talking of self-referential *utterances*, not self-referential *sentences*. (The same sentence can be uttered on many occasions.) We can, following Reichenbach, call the utterance itself a 'token', and this sort of reflexivity 'token-reflexivity'. Tenses can also be eliminated, since such a sentence as 'he will run' can be replaced by 'he *runs* at some future time' (with tenseless 'runs') and hence by 'he *runs* later than this utterance'. Similarly, 'he runs' means 'he *runs* (tenseless) simultaneous with this utterance', and 'he ran' means 'he *runs* (tenseless) earlier than this utterance'.* All the jobs which can be done by tenses can be done by means of the tenseless way of talking and the self-referential utterance 'this utterance'. Of course, every time you use the words 'this utterance' you refer to a different utterance. So though I have just said that 'all the jobs' we can do with tenses and with words such as 'past', 'present', 'future', and 'now' can be done in our tenseless language together with the self-referential utterance 'this utterance', there is nevertheless one sort of thing that we cannot say in our tenseless language. We cannot translate a sentence of the form 'This event was future, is present and will be past'.

So far from this last fact being a criticism of the tenseless way of talking, it is, I think, pure gain. The inability to translate talk of events changing in respect of pastness, presentness, and futurity into our tenseless language can be taken simply as a proof of the concealed token reflexivity of tenses and of words such as 'past', 'present', 'future', and 'now'. If 'past' means 'earlier than this utterance' it is going to have a different reference every time it is used. If uttered in 1950 it refers to events earlier than 1950 and if uttered in 1965 it refers to events earlier than 1965. The notion of events 'changing from future to past' is simply a confused acknow-

---

* H. Reichenbach has given an excellent discussion of tenses and similar notions in terms of 'token-reflexivity' in §§ 50–1 of his *Elements of Symbolic Logic* (Macmillan, New York, 1947).

ledgment of this quite simple sort of fact. Once we see this we banish from the universe much unnecessary mystery.

If past, present, and future were real properties of events, then it would require explanation that an event which becomes present in 1965 becomes present at that date and not at some other (and this would have to be an explanation over and above the explanation of why an event of this sort *occurred* in 1965). Indeed, every event is 'now' at some time or another, and so the notion of 'now' cannot be that of an objective property in nature which singles out some events from others. When we talk in our four-dimensional language of space–time we must clearly talk neither of events nor of things changing, since we have replaced the notion of a thing as the permanent in change by that of a four-dimensional entity, some of whose time slices *are* or *are* not different from others. But even in our language of the permanent in change we must still not think of *events* changing. Things (and processes) come into existence, change, or stay the same, whereas to say that an event (such as the beginning of a football match) 'came into existence' or 'changed' would be absurd. The only exception to this rule is that we *can* say that events 'become present', or 'become past', or even 'become probable' or 'become unlikely'. (On the other hand, it is somewhat strained to say that a *thing* becomes past or probable.) These phenomena of language can be neatly explained once we recognise the fact that utterances of words such as 'past', 'present', and 'future' refer to themselves. So also with 'probable' and 'unlikely', since here 'probable' and 'unlikely' mean 'probable, or unlikely, in terms of *present* evidence'.

Some philosophers have talked as though events 'become' or 'come into existence'. 'Become' is a transitive verb, and so to say that an event 'becomes' must presumably mean that it 'becomes present', and this, we have seen, misleads by concealing the token-reflexivity of 'present' and suggesting that the becoming present of an event is a real change like, for example, the becoming brown of a grassy hillside in summer. Similarly, an event cannot come into existence—a new building can come into existence, but the building of it cannot meaningfully be said to come into existence. (In the four-dimensional way of talking, of course, we must not say even that *things* come into existence—we replace talk of a building coming into existence at *t* by talk of the earliest time slice of the building *being* at *t*.) Some philosophers have erected these misconceptions about the grammar of the verbs 'to become' and 'to come into existence' into a metaphysics, as when, for example, Whitehead said that 'actual occasions become'.

We can also see how misleading it is to talk of the flow of time, or of our advance through time. To say that by next year a year of time will have gone by is simply to say that our conscious experiences of a year later than this utterance *are* (tenseless) a year later than this utterance. Our consciousness does not literally advance into the future, because if it did we could intelligibly ask 'How fast does it advance?' We should need to postulate a hyper-time with reference to which our advance in time could be measured (seconds per hyper-seconds), but there seems to be no reason to postulate such an entity as a hyper-time. (There is still something odd about movement in time even if it is said, as it might be, that the hyper-time has an *order* but no metric. This would rule out talk of 'seconds per hyper-seconds', but it would not affect the fact that change in time would still be a change with respect to hyper-time. Moreover, anyone who thought that time-flow was necessary for time would presumably want to say that hyper-time-flow was necessary for hyper-time. He would therefore be driven to postulate a hyper-hyper-time, and so on without end.)

It is true that sometimes in relativity theory it is said that time 'runs more slowly' in a moving system than it does in a system at rest relative to us. This, however, is not to imply any movement or 'running' of time. What is meant, by this misleading locution, is that according to the conventions of simultaneity of our system of axes the space–time interval between events on our clock is greater than that between simultaneous events on a clock in the moving system. Equally, since we are moving relative to the other system, clocks in our system 'run slow' relative to the moving system. Indeed, so far from relativity leading to difficulties for us, the reverse is the case. The four-dimensional way of talking which we have advocated could still have been possible in pre-relativity days, but it has derived additional theoretical advantages from Minkowski's discovery that the Lorentz transformations of special relativity can be regarded simply as a rotation of axes in space–time. This is not the place to go into an exposition of relativity, but I wish to record the conviction that many of the puzzles and paradoxes of relativity (or rather those things which are sometimes wrongly thought to be puzzles and paradoxes) can most easily be resolved by drawing diagrams of Minkowski space–time, in which most of these at first sight counter-intuitive facts will at once look quite obvious. (We must, of course, bear in mind that the geometry of space–time is not Euclidean.)

If I am right in supposing that 'now' is equivalent to 'simultaneous with this utterance', then I am able, as we have seen, to reject the notion of an objective 'now', the notion that even in past ages when there were perhaps no sentient beings there was nevertheless a moment which was distinguishable as 'the present' or 'now'.* An utterance of the word 'now' refers to itself, since it refers to the set of events simultaneous with itself. Now the special theory of relativity shows that there is no unique set of events which is 'now' or 'simultaneous with this utterance'. Which time slice of the four-dimensional manifold constitutes a 'now' depends on the frame of reference in which we are at rest. Our four-dimensional cake can be sliced at different angles. It is worth mentioning this consideration, since I have known one very eminent disciple of Whitehead (and therefore of an objective 'becoming') to have been genuinely worried by it. For our purposes we can easily modify the notions of 'now' or 'present' to mean 'simultaneous, relative to the utterer's frame of reference, of this utterance'. Similar modifications must be made for 'past' and 'future'.

The notions of 'past', 'present', and 'future' are more complex than those of 'earlier' and 'later', since the former notions do, and the latter notions do not, involve reference to the utterer's position in space–time. 'Earlier' and 'later' fit into the tenseless locution that I have advocated, whereas 'past', 'present', and 'future' do not.

It may now be objected: 'So much the worse for the tenseless way of talking.' For it may be said that so far from the tensed language being definable in terms of the tenseless one (together with the notion of self-referential utterances), the tenseless '*is*' has

---

* See the passage from H. Bergmann, *Der Kampf um das Kausalgesetz in der jüngsten Physik* (Braunschweig, 1929), pp. 27–8, which is quoted in A. Grünbaum's paper 'Carnap's Views on the Foundations of Geometry', in P. A. Schilpp (ed.), *The Philosophy of Rudolf Carnap* (Open Court, La Salle, Illinois, 1963). Grünbaum's paper contains an excellent critique of the idea of an objective 'now'.

to be defined in terms of the tensed one. As Wilfrid Sellars has objected,* a tenseless sentence 'x is ϕ at t' is equivalent to the tensed one 'Either x was ϕ at t or is ϕ at t or will be ϕ at t'. So 'x *is* ϕ at t' is not like '7 *is* a prime number', which does *not* mean '7 was, is, or will be a prime number'.

Now there is, I agree, a difference between 'x *is* ϕ at t' and '7 *is* a prime number'. But it does not appear to be happily expressed by saying that the former sentence is not really tenseless. It is better expressed by saying that '*is* a prime number at such and such a time' is not a meaningful predicate. The difference can be brought out within the *predicates* of 'x *is* ϕ at t' and '7 *is* a prime number' and has nothing to do with the copula. It is true that in extending the tenseless way of talking from pure mathematics to discourse about the space–time world it is natural to introduce 'x *is* ϕ at t' via the locution 'x was, is, or will be ϕ at t'. This is because it is tacitly agreed that x is a space–time entity and so earlier, simultaneous with or later than our present utterance, though in the present context which it is does not matter. But though it is natural to wean users of tensed language from their tenses in this way, it is by no means logically necessary that a tenseless language should be introduced in this manner.

A fable may be of use here. Consider a tribe whose religious and social life depended on the exact numerical age in years of the king, and that for this reason their very language made a difference between three sorts of numbers: those numbers which were less than the number of years which was the king's age, the number which was equal to this number, and the numbers which were greater than this number. Indeed, our tribe do not think of the three sorts of numbers as numbers, but believe that there are three sort of entities, alphas, betas, and gammas. They are, of course, slightly puzzled that every year (until the king dies) a gamma becomes a beta and a beta becomes an alpha. Someone might get the bright idea of introducing the notion of number as 'number = alpha or beta or gamma'. Would this show that the notion of 'number' had anything to do with the age of the king? It has indeed been introduced by reference to notions that have to do with the age of the king, but in such a way that this kingly

* In his essay, 'Time and the World Order', in H. Feigl and G. Maxwell (eds.), *Minnesota Studies in the Philosophy of Science*, Vol. III (University of Minnesota Press, 1962), pp. 527–616, see p. 533.

reference 'cancels out'. Sellars argues that Tom, in 1955, Dick, in 1956, and Harry, in 1957, could agree that Eisenhower should be (tenselessly) President in 1956, but that their reasons would be different. Tom's reason would be 'Eisenhower will be President in 1956', Dick's reason would be 'Eisenhower is President in 1956', and Harry's reason would be 'Eisenhower was President in 1956'. These considerations, says Sellars, make it quite clear that the tenseless present, introduced via 'was, is, or will be', is quite other than the tenseless present of mathematics. As against this, I would say this: the fact that, since they speak from different temporal perspectives, Tom, Dick, and Harry give different reasons for saying 'Eisenhower *is* (tenseless) President in 1956' does not show that they mean anything non-tenseless. For a reason '*q*' offered for '*p*' in the explanation '*p* because *q*', may well contain extraneous and irrelevant elements. It does not therefore seem to me that Sellars has given any convincing reason for saying that there is any important difference between the tenseless '*is*' of 'Eisenhower *is* President in 1956' and '7 + 5 *is* equal to 12'. Of course Eisenhower is a temporal entity, and so 'in 1956' has sense in relation to him, and numbers are non-temporal entities, and so there is no question of 'in 1956' in the case of the second proposition. This distinction can perfectly well be made explicit in the *predicates* of the two sentences and need not be done in the *copulae*. This also explains why it is natural (though there is no need to suppose that it is logically *necessary*) to introduce the tenseless *is* in the case of 'Eisenhower *is* President in 1956' *via* the idiom 'was, is, or will be', whereas it would, as Sellars notes, not be natural to do so in cases like '7 + 5 *is* equal to 12'.

A sentence of the form '*x* is *φ* at *t*' is, of course, not timeless, any more than '*x* is *φ* at such and such a place at *t*' is *spaceless*. Timelessness is not the same as tenselessness. '7 *is* a prime number' is both tenseless and timeless. (There is no sense in saying '7 *is* a prime number at *t*'.) The tenseless way of talking does not therefore imply that physical things or events are eternal in the way in which the number 7 is.

As we have already noted, it is sometimes said that 'this utterance' is to be analysed as 'the utterance which is *now*'. If so, of course, tenses or the notions of past, present, and future *are* fundamental. My reply to this move is to say that this is simply a dogmatic rejection of the analysis in terms of token-reflexiveness. On this analysis 'now' is elucidated in terms of 'this utterance', and not vice-versa. This seems to me to be a perfectly legitimate procedure. How does one settle the argument with someone who says that 'this utterance' has to be analysed in terms of 'utterance now'? Any analysis is a way of looking at language, and there is no one way. I advocate my way, because it fits our ordinary way of talking much more closely to our scientific way of looking at the world and it avoids unnecessary mystification. If someone is adamant that his analysis is the correct analysis of ordinary language I am prepared to concede him this rather empty point. Ordinary language is, then, on his account, more at variance with science than is my version of ordinary language. Nevertheless, the two analyses are in practice pretty well equivalent: in ordinary life a linguist will detect no difference between 'ordinary language', as in accordance with my analysis, and 'ordinary language', as in accordance with my opponent's analysis. Our ordinary language is just not quite so 'ordinary' as is our opponent's, but it is just as good even for ordinary purposes. It is perhaps more 'ordinary' to say that sugar 'melts' than that it 'dissolves', but the greater scientific correctness of the latter locution does not in any way unfit it for even the most practical purposes. Similarly, the additional theoretical advantages of looking at temporal language in the present way suggest that we should prefer this analysis to the other. Perhaps the objector is saying that the present analysis is impossible for any language, whether 'ordinary' or scientific. But it is not at all evident why the objector should think that an utterance like 'this utterance' cannot be *directly* self-referential. We hear a token of the form 'this utterance' and simply understand that this token utterance is the one referred to. We can at a later date *say* what the utterance referred to was: we can enumerate sufficient of its characteristics to identify it. It is always logically possible, of course, that some *other* utterance should possess this list of characteristics—we can misidentify an utterance just as we can misidentify a stone, a tree, or a person. But in fact we need not and do not. Moreover, if we *did* misidentify it, how would the proposal to elucidate 'this' in terms of 'now' have prevented us?

The self-reference of specific utterances of words such as 'here' and 'now' is sufficient to deal with the following puzzle: it is logically possible that in remote regions of space–time the universe might repeat itself exactly.* We cannot therefore uniquely single out an entity (say this table) by referring to it by means of some set of properties—elsewhere in the universe there might be another table with exactly the same qualities and relations to other objects. A token-reflexive expression can, however, uniquely pick out this table—'this table is near the utterance of *this token*'. Of course there may well be other Smarts in other regions of space–time uttering precisely similar tokens, but they can all refer uniquely to their environments by token-reflexive means. There is, however, no need for words such as 'now' or tenses—'this utterance' or 'this token' is always enough to do the trick. Sellars makes a similar point when he argues that token-reflexives are needed to distinguish the real world from fictional worlds. (The real world is a system of entities which includes *this*.) There are obvious difficulties here, which perhaps can be got round only if one accepts Sellars' own interesting but debatable views on the concept of existence. I should wish to say too, however, that tenses and words such as 'present' or 'now' are unimportant here, and that a simple token-reflexive device (corresponding to 'this utterance') is enough to do the trick. For cosmological *theory*, moreover, token-reflexivity is *not* needed. Here one can simply assert, as part of the theory, either that the universe repeats itself in remote parts of space–time or that it does not. It is only in *applying* the theory to observations that unique references have actually to be made.

It should be hardly necessary, at this stage, I should hope, to emphasise that when in the tenseless way of talking we banish tenses, we really must banish them. Thus, when we say that future events exist we do *not* mean that they exist now (present tense). The view of the world as a four-dimensional manifold does not therefore imply that, as some people seem to have thought, the future is already 'laid up'. To say that the future is already laid up is to say that future events exist *now*, whereas when I say of future events that they *exist* (tenselessly) I am doing so simply because, in this case, they *will* exist. The tensed and tenseless locutions are like oil and water—they do not mix, and if you try to mix them you get into needless trouble. We can now see also that the view of the world as a space–time manifold no more implies determinism

* See A. W. Burks, 'A Theory of Proper Names', *Philosophical Studies*, Vol. 2, 1951, pp. 36–45, and N. L. Wilson, 'The Identity of Indiscernibles and the Symmetrical Universe', *Mind*, Vol. 62, 1953, pp. 506–11.

than it does the fatalistic view that the future 'is already laid up'. It is compatible both with determinism and with indeterminism, *i.e.* both with the view that earlier time slices of the universe are determinately related by laws of nature to later time slices and with the view that they are not so related.

When we use tenses and token-reflexive words such as 'past', 'present', and 'future' we are using a language which causes us to see the universe very much from the perspective of our position in space–time. Our view of the world thus acquires a certain anthropocentricity, which can best be eliminated by passing to a tenseless language. By the use of such expressions as 'earlier than this utterance' and 'later than this utterance' we make quite explicit the reference to our particular position in space–time. Once we recognise this anthropocentric reference and bring it out into the open we are less likely to project it on to the universe. The tenseless and minimally token-reflexive language enables us to see the world, in Spinoza's phrase, *sub specie aeternitatis*.

THE TEMPORAL ASYMMETRY OF THE WORLD

We have rejected the notions of 'time flow' and of 'absolute becoming'. We conceive of the universe as a space–time manifold. We may now be struck by a puzzling fact. Why is it that the universe seems to be asymmetrical in the time direction, whereas, on a large scale, it seems to be quite symmetrical in the various space directions?* For example, there are photographs, fossil records, footprints in sand, and innumerable other such species of traces of the past, and yet nothing at all comparable in the case of the future. We know a great deal about past history and yet the future is obscure to us. In some cases, of course, we can predict the future, just as we can retrodict the past, but this does not affect the present issue, since our knowledge through traces greatly exceeds that which we should get through retrodiction alone. Human memories themselves provide a special case of the concept of a trace, since

* Though the world may be asymmetrical as regards *reflections*. This is suggested by the recent discovery in physics that parity is not conserved. In an article 'The Temporal Asymmetry of the World', *Analysis*, Vol. 14, 1953–54, pp. 79–83, I asserted the asymmetry of the world with regard to rotations, but this was due to elementary confusion of thought on my part, and not to prescience of the discovery about parity!

they presumably arise from traces in the neurophysiological structure of the brain.

The question of why the universe is asymmetrical in this way, of why there seems to be nothing analogous to traces of future events, is one which the adherent of time flow or of 'objective becoming' may fail to find puzzling. For he may relate it to the alleged fact that 'time flows one way' or may say that 'there can be traces of the past because past events exist, whereas there cannot be traces of future events because they have not come into existence yet'. We have seen reason to reject this sort of talk. Happily, however, our puzzle is soluble, and soluble in an illuminating scientific manner rather than by means of the facile devices of the *a priori* metaphysician. The solution of this problem is one of the most fascinating chapters in recent scientific philosophy, and the most up-to-date discussion of it will be found in some of the recent writings of A. Grünbaum.* Important contributions are those by H. Reichenbach,† E. Schrödinger,‡ and others. An important suggestion on different lines is by K. R. Popper.§

The directionality which puzzles us does not show up in the laws of classical mechanics, electromagnetism, or in quantum mechanics. Any solution of these laws of the form $f(t)$ has a corresponding solution $f(-t)$. However, as K. R. Popper has shown,‖ even in classical mechanics and electromagnetism a directionality becomes apparent if besides the *laws* we consider *boundary conditions*. Consider a spherical light wave emitted from a point in space, for example from an electric bulb. The equations of propagation of the spherical wave are certainly unchanged by a transformation from t to $-t$. In other words, a train of spherical waves *converging* to a point is equally compatible with the laws of nature. Nevertheless, as Popper points out, the initial conditions for the second

* *Op. cit.* See also his 'The Nature of Time', in R. Colodny (ed.), *Frontiers of Science and Philosophy* (University of Pittsburgh Press, 1962).

† *The Direction of Time* (Cambridge University Press, 1957).

‡ 'Irreversibility', *Proceedings of the Royal Irish Academy*, Vol. 52, 1950, pp. 189–95.

§ *Nature*, Vol. 177, 1956, p. 538. See also the letters by E. L. Hill and A. Grünbaum, and reply by Popper, *Nature*, Vol. 179, 1957, pp. 1296–7, and Grünbaum's paper 'Popper on Irreversibility', in *The Critical Approach, Essays in Honor of Karl Popper,* edited by M. Bunge (The Free Press, New York, 1964).

‖ See previous footnote.

interpretation are quite improbable. Rays of light would have to be sent out from all points on a sphere of a radius of cosmic dimensions, the rays of light travelling along radii of the sphere towards its centre. Though such a combination of occurrences would be compatible with the laws of nature, it would constitute an infinitely improbable coincidence. There would have to be a most unlikely harmonising of emissions from the points of the sphere so as to simulate in reverse a spherical wave emitted from a point. Some extraordinary hypothesis would be needed to account for such a queer thing. When, on the other hand, we consider the spherical wave emitted from a lamp we do not have to postulate any improbable initial conditions. Moreover, the rays converging from a distant sphere would still not come from infinity.

In some cases, therefore, we can give an account of temporal asymmetry without going beyond the differential equations of classical physics, together with a consideration of boundary conditions. The consideration of boundary conditions involves us in probability considerations. For a widely applicable explanation of temporal asymmetry, however, we must pass to thermodynamics and statistical mechanics. Notice that here again probability plays a central role. For example, consider a chamber divided into two compartments A and B. In A is a gas at temperature θ_1, and in B is a gas at temperature θ_2. When the partition between the chambers is removed the gases mix and settle down to a temperature intermediate between θ_1 and θ_2. It is, of course, conceivable that on the average the faster-moving molecules stayed in A and the slower-moving ones stayed in B, but statistics show that this would be almost infinitely improbable. For this reason also we never observe that a gas at temperature θ_3 separates spontaneously into two spatially distinct gases at different temperatures θ_1 and θ_2 respectively. An important objection has, however, been raised against this reasoning, and it will be helpful to consider it. This is the 'reversibility objection'. It goes as follows. According to gas theory, the probability of a molecule's having a velocity v in a certain direction is equal to the probability of its having a velocity $-v$ in that direction (*i.e.* a velocity v in the *opposite* direction). Now if all the velocities of the molecules of the gas at temperature θ_3 were reversed we should get the opposite process to our mixing process above, and the gases would separate out into the two parts A and B at temperature θ_1 and θ_2. That is, contrary to what was asserted above, separation processes must be as common as mixing processes.

Kinetic theory, of the sort we are considering in connection with the reversibility objection, presupposes that we are dealing with a closed and finite system of particles. In order therefore to apply these considerations to the universe as a whole let us make the assumption that the universe contains a finite number of particles, that there is no creation or annihilation of matter, and that the universe is not expanding or contracting. These assumptions are contrary to what is probably the case, but it is nevertheless instructive here to suppose that they hold good. With these assumptions it is possible to talk of the entropy (roughly the amount of disorganisation) of the universe as a whole. The entropy of the universe is increasing much as the disorder of a pack of cards increases as they are shuffled. When the shuffling reaches completion the universe is in its 'heat death': there is no order anywhere, such as is exemplified by hot sun and cold earth, but everywhere there is a flat uniformity. A pack of cards, if it is shuffled for long enough, will emerge from a state of randomness back into a state in which the cards are arranged in suits. Similarly, if the universe were finite and non-expanding its entropy curve would ultimately begin to descend again. Instead of increasing, entropy would begin to decrease. This illustrates the theorem that reversed states are as probable as non-reversed ones.

Let us consider the part of the entropy curve of the universe in which we ourselves are. (Remember that we are assuming for the sake of argument that it is legitimate to speak in this way of the entropy of the universe as a whole.) Now, as Reichenbach points out, we are not in practice concerned with the entropy of the whole universe: it is something of which we can have no knowledge. There are, however, vast numbers of what Reichenbach calls 'branch systems': such a system is one whose state of disorder 'branches' off from that of a wider system, and which remains relatively isolated until it merges with the wider system again. For example, consider a footprint on a beach. The state of order of the grains of sand that make up the footprint is greater than it was before the footprint was imprinted. This is compatible with the law that entropy, or disorder, always increases, because of the more than compensating increase of the entropy of the man who makes the footprints and is metabolically depleted as he walks.

Ultimately as a result of wind and weather the footprint will merge into the flatness of the beach again, and its entropy level will return to that of the wider system. Another example of a branch system is exemplified by blocks of ice in a beaker of water which gradually melt and return to the temperature of the surroundings. Written and fossil records, magnetic tapes and photographic plates, all provide further examples of branch systems. In these cases it is useful, following Reichenbach, to talk of macroentropy, for we are primarily concerned with the states of order or disorder of entities much larger than molecules, such as grains of sand and pieces of print. Macroentropy is analogous to, and of course ultimately reducible to, microentropy, the state of disorder of assemblages of molecules, such as is considered in statistical mechanics.

Branch systems, we have noted, return ultimately to the entropy curve of the universe (on the assumption, as before, that we can meaningfully talk of the entropy of the whole universe). Now all branch systems with which we are acquainted run in the same direction. These provide a background against which we can test the direction of any particular process. A process is in the direction of positive time if it is in the direction of increase of entropy of branch systems, for example if it begins when ice *is* put into a beaker and finishes when the ice *is* melted. (It would, of course, have been more idiomatic if I had said 'when the ice has melted', but I have stuck to the tenseless 'is' in order to dodge unwarranted accusations of circularity.)

Now consider a finite non-expanding universe which ultimately attains its heat death, after which its entropy curve will run on a downgrade. In the era of the universe which is on the far side of the heat death branch systems will point the opposite way to branch systems in our era. Intelligent beings who lived in this era would get an illusion of time flow which is the opposite of ours.

Some philosophers have thought that a universe in which the direction of positive time went the other way would be a 'crazy' or 'irrational' world. As F. H. Bradley put it: 'Death would come before birth, the blow would follow the wound, and all must seem irrational.'* Similarly, J. N. Findlay has characterised such a world as one 'where a ripple would first form on the edge of a pond, and then swell steadily towards the centre, to be followed

* *Appearance and Reality*, 2nd Ed. (Oxford University Press, 1930), p. 190.

by a set of even larger, converging ripples, until on the arrival of the last, largest ripple at the centre, a stone would emerge with sudden noise, leaving the water behind it miraculously still. Or where a set of foot-prints would become more and more clear-cut with the lapse of time, until they were ultimately walked upon (and blotted out) by some suitable creature moving in reverse.'* Findlay says that such a world 'wouldn't strike us as queer but definitely crazy'. I contend, on the contrary, that the 'backwards' universe would both be and seem just like our 'forwards' universe. For one thing, our intuitive sense of time direction presumably is causally explicable by reference to the accumulation of memory traces in our brains. As A. Grünbaum has said, 'The flux of time consists in the *instantaneous awarenesses* of *both* the temporal order *and* the *diversity* of the membership of the set of remembered (recorded) or forgotten events, awarenesses in each of which the instant of its own occurrence constitutes a *distinguished element*'†". It is difficult to believe that our intuitive sense of the direction of time does not arise from the formation of memory traces in our brain, which constitute 'branch systems'. Ignoring for the moment the possibility of the obliteration of memory traces, it is the case that in our world if time t_1 is earlier than time t_2 we have more memories at t_2 than at t_1. It is not surprising that we get the feeling of the advance of time as like the mercury running up a thermometer tube, though in fact what is changing is not time but the stock of our memory traces. Now in the reversed universe if t_1 is earlier than t_2 (according to our reckoning) there will be more memory traces in a person of that universe at t_1 than at t_2. Such a person will feel as though time is flowing in the direction from t_2 to t_1. So far from his world seeming crazy or irrational it will seem to him exactly as our world does to us. If an era of the universe in which its entropy curve is on the upgrade is followed by one in which the entropy curve is on a downgrade there is complete symmetry between the two eras. Indeed, from the point of view of someone in the other era he is on the upgrade and our era follows his and is on a downgrade.

We have, of course, made the artificial assumption of a non-expanding universe with a fixed and finite number of particles in it.

* J. N. Findlay, review of C. Ehrenfels' *Cosmogony*, in *Philosophy*, Vol. 25, 1950, pp. 346–7.

† 'Carnap's Views on the Foundations of Geometry', *op. cit.* p. 663.

On other assumptions there would not be symmetrically opposed eras. However, we have seen enough to understand that the temporal asymmetry of the universe (or at the least of our own cosmic era) comes not from the nature of time itself, but from very general facts, largely of a statistical sort, about the things in the universe. These facts can perfectly well be expressed within the theory of the universe as a space–time manifold.*

CONCLUSION

In this chapter I have been defending the view of the world as a four-dimensional system of entities in space–time. Concepts such as 'past' and 'future' have been shown to be anthropocentric in that they relate to particular human utterances. My advocacy of the four-dimensional picture of the world is therefore, among other things, part of the same campaign against anthropocentricity and romanticism in metaphysics that I have been waging elsewhere, as in the chapters on secondary qualities, consciousness, and man as a mechanism. It is surely no accident that romantic, vitalistic, and anti-mechanistic philosophies such as those of Bergson and Whitehead are also those which lay great emphasis on the alleged transitory aspect of time, process or absolute becoming. While I concede that our present notions of space and time may perhaps have to be revised, the idea of the world as a space–time manifold is nearer the truth than these romantic and obscure philosophical theories.

* For a critique of theories of time flow and of 'absolute becoming', together with a defence of the view of the universe as a space–time manifold, the reader may be further referred to Donald Williams' excellent article, 'The Myth of Passage', *Journal of Philosophy*, Vol. 48, 1951, pp. 457–72.

VIII

MAN AND NATURE

IF you look at the world through blue spectacles everything will look blue, but blue things will not stand out from one another in their blueness. In the same sort of way our ordinary manner of talking about the world is suffused with concepts which relate the things in the world to our human concerns and interests, and which depend, in often unnoticed ways, on our human physiology and our particular station in space–time. In particular, we saw in Chapter VII that this was so with our tensed language and our references to past, present, and future. If the anthropocentricity inherent in these concepts is not brought out into the open we can have a misleading picture of the world. We think, for example, of objective colour *qualia* or of an objective *now*, much as the Hebrews looked up at the dome of the sky and thought that this was a solid half-spherical shell, or *firmament*, and did not realise that this apparently solid object was an illusion of their own perspective.

It is perhaps useful at this stage to consider the possibility of a 'cosmic language', such as has been devised by H. Freudenthal. Freudenthal has addressed himself to the problem of devising a method whereby we might communicate with rational beings on another planet, perhaps a planet of some distant star. We can neglect, for present purposes, the *practical* difficulties in such a project. One of these is that such communication would be very slow. Thus, one would have to wait forty years for a reply to a radio or light signal sent to a comparatively near star twenty light years distance from us. We can also neglect the details of the ingenious method by which Freudenthal proposes to develop his language (called 'Lincos') in such a way that the distant rational beings can come to guess its meaning. For these the reader is referred to Freudenthal's writings.* For our purposes let us simply consider the possibility that such a language has been devised.

We can make use of this supposition to illustrate a distinction between two sorts of anthropocentricity. These two sorts of anthropocentricity differ in accordance with whether we take 'anthropos' or 'man' to mean 'rational being', in which case there could be 'men' on distant planets, or as to whether we take 'anthropos' or 'man' to refer to members of the terrestrial species *homo sapiens*. The latter, but not necessarily the former, sort of anthropocentricity can be brought out by considering how our notions could be expressed in a cosmic language. Thus, our colour words tempt us to an anthropocentricity of the latter sort: concepts which depend on the idiosyncracies of the neurophysiology of *homo sapiens* can easily be thought to have a cosmic significance. But if we were to attempt to translate our colour vocabulary into a cosmic language we should have to bring this anthropocentricity out into the open by defining colours in terms of the reactions of a normal human percipient. This would be of little interest to our friends on the distant planet. Not having a normal human percipient handy, they would not be able to test whether a flower found on their planet was, say, purple. Of course, assuming the truth of the three-colour theory of vision, they could be told by us what sort of device using three different photo-electric cells would be equivalent to the human colour-vision system. Using this device, they could test whether their flower was 'purple'. Nevertheless, this would seem to be a rather pointless procedure!

The other sort of anthropocentricity can be illustrated by the tendency of tenses and of words such as 'past', 'present', and 'future' to bemuse us with the idea of an objective 'now'. This sort of trouble might persist even in a cosmic language, which might conceivably contain tenses and the like. (Though in practice it probably would not, if we consider the fact that the transmission of the word 'now' and its reception would very likely be many

---

* H. Freudenthal, *Lincos, Design of a Language for Cosmic Intercourse, Part I* (North-Holland, Amsterdam, 1960). Freudenthal has also given a very readable popular account of his project in an article, 'Towards a cosmic language', *Delta* (Netherlands), summer 1958.

years apart. Moreover, there would be relativistic difficulties connected with the variation between our conventions of simultaneity and those of our friends in the distant planet, since if this was a planet of a remote star it might have a considerable proper motion relative to us. The logical grammar of tenses would have to be more complex than in our purely terrestrial language.) Similarly, rational beings on a distant planet might have the same temptations as we have, to think of themselves as apart from nature, and not merely complicated physical mechanisms.

In spite of the fact, noted in the last paragraph, that one sort of anthropocentricity could persist even in users of a cosmic language, it is still a valuable exercise to philosophers to consider how much of what they want to say about the world could be translated into a cosmic language. If anything cannot be so translated they are certainly not seeing the world impartially or *sub specie aeternitatis*.

Kant's so-called Copernican revolution was really an anti-Copernican counter-revolution. Just when man was being taken away from the centre of things by the astronomers, and when he was soon to be put in his biological place by the theory of evolution, Kant was, by means of his metaphysics, putting him back in the centre again. It is a major theme of this book to oppose this Kantian tendency, and to try to show that philosophical clarity helps us, just as scientific knowledge does, to see the world in a truly objective way and to see that man is in no sense at the centre of things. Nor is man set over against nature. Man is part of nature, a very wonderful part of nature perhaps, but not necessarily pre-eminent in any way. The vast astronomical spaces frighten men, and philosophical anti-Copernicans are therefore found congenial. It is better, however, to face reality and see the world truly as it is. Many romantic philosophies have perhaps had their emotional source in human vanity, which may even make us blind to fallacies and implausibilities. To see man in relation to the universe at large is also very salutary for our thinking about ethics, for which a sense of proportion and of our own littleness and non-uniqueness cannot do any harm. This leads on to the question of whether our physicalist metaphysics has any implication for conduct.

MATERIALISM AND VALUES

The philosophical view presented in this book may correctly be described as materialistic. Some people seem to think that such a philosophy must be morally pernicious, that a materialistic metaphysics must be incompatible with a humane and unselfish ethics. I shall try to show that this is not so. There is, of course, a popular sense of the word 'materialist' in which to call a man a materialist *is* to make an adverse moral judgment about him. To be a materialist in this sense is to be concerned only with the pursuit of wealth, power, luxury, and entertainment. A materialist in this sense is someone who is interested in things only because they will bring him certain sorts of gratification. Whether a person is a materialist in the metaphysical sense, which has to do not with his interests and gratifications but with his beliefs about the cosmos, is irrelevant to whether or not he is a materialist in the popular sense. Indeed, a materialist in the popular sense may have no considered beliefs about the cosmos. He will not be interested in the cosmos. His thought will tend towards such things as motor cars and television sets, beefsteaks and burgundy. A metaphysical materialist may well be ascetic in his habits: he may be too interested in philosophy and physics and biology to care very much for his creature comforts. Nor is there any reason why a metaphysical materialist should not have a compassionate interest in the well-being of his fellow creatures. Indeed, there may even be some reason for supposing that metaphysical materialism may be psychologically conducive to a humane and kindly ethic. If a man genuinely thinks of himself and other men as very complicated machines he will nevertheless feel that these are very wonderful machines. A human being has a complexity and subtlety of internal structure which is incomparably greater than that of an aeroplane or a clock. A man who has any feeling at all for machinery will be extremely reluctant to destroy even an aeroplane or a clock. And yet there are men who think nothing of burying an axe or a bullet in the beautifully organised brain of a fellow creature.

A really brutal person will not be influenced either way by metaphysical consideration. On the other hand, there are civilised and far from brutal men who are far too willing to consider the destruction of millions of their fellow creatures in war. Some men have even calmly considered the possible destruction of all life on earth, forgetting how remote our present ideological disputes would seem to our more highly evolved descendants (if we have any descendants) of millions of years hence. A metaphysical dualist may be far too tempted to think: 'Bombs can destroy the body, but they cannot destroy the soul.' Many of the excesses of the Spanish Inquisition were thought to be justified by the belief that the victims' sufferings on earth were justifiable as a warning which might prevent incomparably more prolonged torments in another world. There is therefore some reason for believing that the dissemination of a materialistic metaphysics might indeed lead to a more kindly and humane ethics in practice. However, we must not take this consideration too far, for most of the misdeeds of men are quite independent of any metaphysical beliefs that they may have.

How can a materialist defend such a humane and beneficent ethic? In the last resort his ethics must depend on what he wants, on how he feels about things. Indeed, in view of the apparent impossibility of deducing 'ought' from 'is',* which was perhaps first clearly pointed out by Hume, we should see that any ethics must ultimately depend on feeling. Even the religious man will accept the precepts of his religion only because either he loves God or because he fears punishment. Hume wrote as follows:

> In every system of morality which I have hitherto met with, I have always remarked, that the author proceeds for some time in the ordinary way of reasoning, and establishes the being of a God, or makes observations concerning human affairs; when of a sudden I am surprised to find, that instead of the usual copulations of propositions, *is*, and *is not*, I meet with no proposition that is not connected with an *ought*, or an *ought not*. This change is imperceptible; but is, however, of the last consequence. For as this *ought*, or *ought not*, expresses some new relation or affirmation, it is necessary that it should be observed and explained; and at the same time that

---

* For a modern and very subtle discussion of this point, see R. M. Hare, *The Language of Morals* (Oxford University Press, 1952). The view that one cannot deduce an 'ought' from an 'is' requires some qualification, however. For example, if P is an 'is' proposition and Q is an 'ought' proposition we can clearly deduce from P the 'ought' proposition 'P or Q'. For a discussion of the qualifications that need to be made, see A. N. Prior, 'The Autonomy of Ethics', *Australasian Journal of Philosophy*, Vol. 38, 1960, pp. 199–206. It will be seen that they are unimportant in the present connection.

a reason should be given, for what seems altogether inconceivable, how this new relation can be a deduction from others, which are entirely different from it. But as authors do not commonly use this precaution, I shall presume to recommend it to the readers; and am persuaded, that this small attention would subvert all the vulgar systems of morality, and let us see that the distinction of vice and virtue is not founded merely on the relations of objects, nor is perceived by reason.*

An analogy may make Hume's essential point clear. Let us compare a moral injunction to a rule of chess, and factual statements, whether about the being of a God, human affairs, or whatever you like, to statements about actual occurrences in a game of chess. It is clear that there is no logical entailment either from a chess rule to a chess move or from a chess move to a chess rule. There is nothing self-contradictory in saying that it is a rule of chess that bishops move diagonally, but that someone had in fact moved his bishop parallel to a side of the board.

No account of scientific facts about the world can by themselves determine what we should do. Some philosophers and scientists have tried to deduce ultimate ethical precepts from the conclusions of evolutionary biology. Thus, it may be pointed out that evolution is tending in the direction from A to B, and it is then suggested that this proves that we should act in certain ways, perhaps by the application of eugenics, so as to help the transition from A to B. The conclusion does not follow. If a man dislikes the prospect of B he may decide to act in such a way as to oppose the transition from A to B. What ethical precepts we recommend depends in the last analysis on what we *want*. Scientific facts alone cannot give us a precept.

This is not to say that scientific facts are not of the greatest importance for ethics. It is simply that scientific facts do not by themselves determine any ethical system. The fact that some event X causes an event Y can be of great importance, but this importance is a secondary one. If we want Y and discover that X causes Y, then we will want X. If, on the other hand, we want *not* to have Y, then we will want not to have X. Taking 'reason' perhaps rather narrowly, as concerned only with facts about the world, we can follow Hume when he said that reason is the slave of the passions.† In order to talk about ethics with other people there

* David Hume, *Treatise of Human Nature*, Book III, Part 1, Section 1.
† *Treatise*, Book II, Part 3, Section 3.

must be some community of interest: we can then go on to argue in what way this interest can most effectively be served. Now among the sort of people with whom *I* want to talk ethics there is a common interest, namely generalised benevolence. There is, among the sort of people with whom I want or am likely to converse, *some* tendency to count oneself neither more nor less than one's fellow men. There is also, I admit, among the sort of people with whom I wish to talk ethics, a tendency to seek exclusively one's own happiness. However, in those cases where seeking one's own happiness does not make for the general happiness, that is in those cases where a person makes others miserable by gratifying his own happiness, these egoistic desires will largely cancel one another out and cannot be made the basis of an interpersonal discussion anyway. We can see, therefore, that generalised benevolence provides at least one possible basis for an ethical system.

I have said that no moral rules can be deduced purely from scientific considerations. Science may be able to tell us what means conduce to what ends, but it cannot tell us what ends to pursue. Nevertheless, the scientific temper can be psychologically conducive to an ethics of generalised benevolence. The scientist tries to find laws of nature which apply anywhere and anywhen, and he will therefore be attracted by a moral outlook which places the interests of all men, whatever their caste or creed, on an equality. He will even be attracted, beyond a merely humanistic ethics, to consider the interests of other species of animal, in so far as these seem capable of happiness or unhappiness, and, if it ever in the future of space technology came to the point where it was of practical importance, he might consider the interests of intelligent extra-terrestrial beings to be as important as his own. There is another reason why scientific thought is psychologically conducive to a widening of ethical interest. A scientist has to attend seriously to the arguments of another scientist, no matter what may be that other scientist's nationality, race, or social position. He must therefore at least respect the other as a source of arguments, and this is psychologically conducive to respecting him as a person in the full sense, and hence to considering his interests equally with one's own.* Of course, there are plenty of cases in

* For some interesting reflections on these lines, see S. I. Benn and R. S. Peters, *Social Principles and the Democratic State* (Allen and Unwin, London, 1959), pp. 31–3.

which this psychological tendency to carry over scientific impartiality to the field of conduct may be outweighed by other factors. In Germany before the war many competent scientists, indeed even some first-rate scientists, were adherents of National Socialism. So far from scientific impartiality being carried over to ethics, it was not carried over even from one field of science to another. Competent physicists have adhered to quite absurd anthropological theories about the races of men.

It is true that many of the men with whom I wish to talk ethics may act not so much from generalized benevolence as from some code of rules of conduct which has simply been drilled into them, or to which they have been drawn by philosophical reasoning about morality. Or perhaps these rules will be accepted because they are laid down by some religion. Against such men there can be two sorts of argument. (Though if their rules do not markedly conflict with the dictates of generalised benevolence I should not much wish to argue against them.) In the first place, if the moral rules stem from a religion it may be possible to argue against the metaphysical basis of the religion. In the second place, one can ask a person if he does not feel the *heartlessness* of putting abstract conformity to a rule before human happiness. Unless the system of rules is equivalent to the system of generalized benevolence there must, at least occasionally, be a conflict between the two systems. Suppose, then, that obeying the rule causes real misery to someone, without compensating advantages to other people. Would it not be cruel to obey the rule?

It is not my purpose here to go further into an exposition and defence of an ethical system. I hope I have said enough to indicate that there is no reason why a philosophical materialist should not have a desire to make people happy, and that this desire provides one possible basis for ethics. A metaphysics which shows man as part of nature, and which quells the overweening pride which makes him think of himself as a spiritual being set over against nature, is likely, in my opinion, to have beneficial results. The concern of this book has, however, not been with whether the system of ideas developed in it is likely to be beneficial, but with whether it is likely to be true.

INDEX

Abduction, 39
Acworth, Richard, 12 n.
Adelaide, vii
After-image, 89, 91–5, 97
Algorithm, 31, 111, 115
Andromeda, 24, 59
Animism, 115
Anthropocentricity, 15, 69, 71, 85–6,
    129, 131–2, 142, 148–51
Anthropology, 156
Aristotle, 7, 92, 131
Armstrong, D. M., vii, 7, 18 n., 22 n.,
    23, 24 n., 74 n., 100
Astronomy, 25, 59–60, 131, 151
Asymmetry, temporal, 142–8
Atoms, 30, 38, 55, 60, 65, 115
Avowals, 91
Axioms, 30–2, 115, 117
Ayer, A. J., 21, 25, 100 n.

Bacteria, 37–8
Baier, K. E. M., 92 n., 98, 100 n.
Bartesaghi, A., vii
Behaviourism, 88–91, 100
Benevolence, 155–6
Benn, S. I., 155 n.
Berenda, C. W., 51 n.
Bergmann, H., 137 n.
Bergson, H., 148
Berkeley, George, 19, 23, 38, 66, 73–4
Biology, 2, 27, 52–64, 151–2, 154
Black, Max, 94 n.
Blame, 126
Bohm, D., 44
Born, Max, 36 n.
Boscovitch, R. G., 45–6, 51
Bouma, P. J., 69, 71 n.
Boyle, R., 55, 84
Bradley, F. H., 146
Bradley, M. C., vii, 83
Brain, 11, 79, 87–8, 91–4, 96–9, 101–6,
    127, 143, 152
Braithwaite, R. B., 28, 33
Branch system, 145–7

Broad, C. D., 132
Broglie, L. de, 38
Brouwer, L. E. J., 6
Brownian motion, 49
Bunge, M., 40 n., 109, 121 n., 143 n.
Burks, A. W., 141 n.

Canonical class, 116
Carroll, Lewis, 4 n., 6
Chance, 12, 58, 123–4
Change, 133, 135
Chemistry, 50–1, 61
Church, A., 115–18, 121
Classes, 14
Colodny, R. G., 40 n., 143 n.
Colour, 47, 64–86, 149–50
Computing machines, 107–21, 123, 128–
    9
Conditionals, 19
Consciousness, 11, 64, 88, 98, 102, 105–
    6, 109, 114, 121, 129, 136, 148
Copenhagen interpretation, 17, 40–1
Copernicus, Copernicans, 40, 48, 131,
    151
Cosmic language, 149–51
Couffignal, L., 108
Craig, William, 29–32
Crime, 122
Cybernetics, 107, 109, 121

Davis, Martin, 112 n.
Dear, G. F., 123
Descartes, R., 106
Determinism, 8, 123–8, 141–2
Deutsch, J. A., 62 n.
Dingle, Herbert, 17, 38
Dodwell, P. C., 62 n.
Double aspect theory, 94
Dream, 20, 33

Ecology, 59
Eddington, A. S., 47
Ehrenfels, C., 147 n.
Einstein, A., 51

Electro-encephalograph, 99
Electromagnetism, 143
Electron, 16–18, 27, 29–31, 33–9, 41–3, 48, 57, 73–4
Electronics, 52–3, 58, 61, 64
Ellis, B. D., 34 n.
Emergence, 50–2, 94
Emory, F. L., 124 n.
Entropy, 145–8
Ethics, 2–3, 151–6
Euclid, 137
Eugenics, 154
Evolution, 2, 13, 53, 59, 67, 131, 151, 154

Farrell, B. A., 62
Fatalism, 141
Feed-back, negative, 69, 102
Feigl, H., 32 n., 37 n., 40 n., 49 n., 68, 91–2, 138 n.
Fermat, P., 112–13
Feyerabend, P. K., 40–1, 48–9
Fictions, theoretical, 33–4, 36, 47
Findlay, J. N., 146–7
Firmament, 149
Flew, A. G. N., vii, 30 n., 126 n.
Free will, 4, 12, 122–4, 126
Frege, G., 14
Freudenthal, H., 149–50
Force, lines of, 33–4, 47
Future, 132–43, 149–50

Galois, E., 120
Gardner, Martin, 9 n.
Geach, P. T., 75 n.
Geiger counter, 123
Gellner, E., 126 n.
Gene, 13, 60, 67
Genesis, 9
Genetics, 50, 56, 58
Gentzen, G., 119
Geology, 9
George, F. H., 120 n.
Germany, 156
God, 3, 4, 19, 46, 131, 153–4
Gödel, K., 31–2, 116–21, 129 n.
Gosse, Philip, 9
Grünbaum, A., 41, 137 n., 143, 147

Haldane, J. B. S., 126 n.
Hallucinations, 20–1, 33
Halsbury, Earl of, 72
Hampshire, Stuart, 16 n., 48 n.
Hare, R. M., 153 n.
Harlow, H. F., 62 n.
Hayek, F. A., 86
Heat death, 145–6
Hebb, D. O., 62 n.
Hebrews, 149
Heisenberg, W., 16

Hempel, C. G., 32 n.
Hill, E. L., 143 n.
Hirst, R. J., 74 n.
Hobart, R. E., 126 n.
Hoffman, Banesh, 44
Hook, Sidney, 92 n., 129 n.
Hormic theory, 115
Hospers, J., 75 n.
Hoyle, F., 54
Hughes, S. E., vii
Hughes, Felicity, vii
Hume, David, 73, 100, 153–4
Hypotheticals, 19

Immortality, 4
Induction, 119–20
Ingenuity, 109, 114–16
Inquisition, Spanish, 153
Interference, 41–3

Jackson, R., 66 n., 84 n.
James, William, 25
Joske, W. D., 92 n.

Kalmus, H., 53 n.
Kant, Immanuel, 45, 151
Kemeny, J. G., 116
Kinetic theory, 40, 57–8, 144–5
Kneale, William, 74

La Mettrie, J. O. de, 107
Land, E. H., 70–1
Landé, A., 41
Laplace, P. S. de, 124
Laws, biological, 50, 52, 60
Laws, physical, 52–8, 60, 124, 143
Legal questions, 110–11, 122
Lewis, C. S., 126 n.
Libertarians, 12–13
Lightning, 93, 101
Lincos, 150
Local signs, 104
Locke, John, 66, 68, 75
Logic, mathematical, 29, 115–19
Logical constructions, 27–8
Lorentz, H. A., 136
Lotze, R. H., 104
Lucas, J. R., 116

McCormack, T. J., 17
McDougall, W., 115
Mace, C. A., 16 n.
Mach, E., 16
Machines, 106–24, 126, 128–9, 152
MacKay, D. M., 102–3, 123 n.
McKinsey, J. C. C., 30
Macroentropy, 146
Malcolm, Norman, 100 n.
Margenau, H., 17

Martin, C. B., vii, 22, 74, 81–3, 101 n.
Matching process, 102
Materialism, 2 n., 152–6
Mathematics, 14, 111–20, 139
Matson, W. I., 61 n.
Maxwell, Grover, 32 n., 36, 40 n., 49 n., 77 n.
Mayo, Bernard, 33, 35
Mays, W., 109
Mechanism, 2, 95, 106–24, 131, 148, 151–2; see also Machines
Medlin, B. H., 100
Melden, A. I., 100 n.
Mendel, G., 53, 56
Mesons, 16
Metalanguage, 117–19
Metaphysics, 3, 136, 148, 151–3
Microscope, 37
Mill, J. S., 17
Milne, E. A., 48
Minkowski, H., 136–7
Minsky, M. L., 114 n.
Molecules, 36–7, 60–1, 67, 144

Nagel, E., 17 n., 51 n., 116
National Socialism, 156
Nations and nationals, 16, 18, 33
Natural history, 53, 57
Naturalism, 3, 126–7
Needham, J., 61 n.
Neumann, J. von, 44
Neutrons, 16–17, 55
Newman, J. R., 116
Newton, Isaac, 51, 55, 59
Nominalism 14–15
Nomological danglers, 68, 90, 94
Nonsense, 3–8
Normal percipient, 77, 79–81
Number, 14, 76, 112, 117, 138–9

Objectivism, 66–9, 71–3, 82
Occam, William of, 11–12, 101
O'Connor, D. J., 125 n.
O'Hair, Gregory, vii

Pain, 89–91, 100, 103–4
Paradox, Russell's, 4–5
Paranoia, 122
Parity, 142 n.
Past, 132–5, 137–43, 148–51
Peirce, C. S., 39
Perception, 102–3
Peters, R. S., 155 n.
Phenomenalism, 15–27, 39, 43
Phlogiston, 38
Photo-electric cell, 71–2, 83–4, 110, 150
Photons, 16, 37–8
Physicalism, 64–5, 68, 83, 88–9, 151
Pitcher, G., 92 n.
Place, U. T., 91–2

Platonism, 14–15
Plausibility, 8–12, 151
Popper, K. R., 5 n., 26, 41, 123, 143
Praise, 126
Predicate calculus, 115–16
Present, 132–5, 137–42, 149–51
Price, H. H., 20, 25
Prior, A. N., 153 n.
Private logic, 99
Probability, 41, 58, 143–5
Protein, 37–8, 61
Protons, 16–17, 30, 36, 38, 48, 55
Psychology, 52, 58, 61–4, 114–15, 129
Psychophysical dualism, 91, 100, 103–4, 153
Ptolemaic theory, 40
Punishment, 122, 124, 126, 153
Purpose, 106–7, 113
Putnam, Hilary, 2 n., 92 n., 98, 128–9

Qualia, 66–8, 71–2, 74–5, 87, 90, 94, 104, 149
Quantum mechanics, 17, 30, 40–4, 46–7, 49, 51, 123, 143
Quine, W. V., 2 n., 13 n., 14 n., 15 n., 129 n.

Ramsey, F. P., 15, 24–5, 28, 33
Reading, 121
Reasons, 126–7
Reception, 102–3
Reductio ad absurdum, 6
Reichenbach, H., 19, 20 n., 92 n., 134, 143, 145–6
Relativity, 74, 130, 136, 151
Religion, 156
Reversibility objection, 144–5
Rosenbloom, P., 116
Russell, Bertrand, 4, 9, 14, 25, 76
Ryle, Gilbert, 26, 48 n., 88–91, 106

Salecker, H., 45
Sartre, J. P., 104 n.
Schilpp, P. A., 137 n.
Schrödinger, E., 143
Secondary qualities, 47, 64–5, 84–6, 88, 148
Sellars, Wilfrid, 23–4, 48, 49 n., 138–9, 141
Sensation reports, 90–2, 97, 99–101, 103
Sensations, bodily, 103–4
Sense data, 25–6, 46, 66–8, 93, 95; see also Sense experiences, Sense impressions
Sense experiences, 2, 18–27, 88–105 passim
Sense impressions, 20–6
Shaffer, Jerome, 98
Smell, 64–5, 84–5
Socrates, 89

Soul, 13, 46, 129
Sound, 64–5, 84–6
Space, 44–6, 96–8, 129–30, 133, 135–42
Spector, M., 39
Spinoza, B., 142
Statistics, 58–60, 144, 148
Stebbing, L. S., 47
Stevenson, J. T., 92 n.
Strang, Colin, 85 n.
Strawson, P. F., 100 n.
Subjectivism, 66, 68–9, 82, 129
Sugar, A. C., 30
Suppes, P., 30
Sutherland, N. S., 62

Taste, 64–5, 85–6
Temperature, 71, 85–6
Tense, 133–4, 137–42, 148–51
Theology, 3, 131
Thermodynamics, 40, 48–9, 55, 68, 71, 144–6
Three-colour theory, 69–72, 150
Time, 44, 129–30, 132–48
Timelessness, 139
Titchener, E. B., 104 n.
Token-reflexivity, 134, 139–42

Truscott, F. W., 124 n.
Turing, A. M., 128–9
Two slit experiment, 41–4

Valency, 37
Values, 152–6
Vartanian, A., 107 n.
Vesey, G. N. A., 104 n.
Vigier, J.-P., 44

Warnock, G. J., 73
Whitehead, A. N., 76, 136–7, 148
Wigner, E. P., 45
Williams, Bernard, vii
Williams, D. C., 72 n., 148 n.
Wilson, N. L., 141 n.
Wisdom, John, 17, 66
Wittgenstein, L., vii, 6, 8 n., 73, 90, 100
Woodger, J. H., 50, 58, 133 n.
Woolsey, C. N., 62 n.
World view, vii, 1–2, 48, 64, 131–2, 148–51

Zermelo, E., 5 n.
Ziff, Paul, 98
Zimmerman, E. J., 44–5